an **avocado** a day

an avocado a day

More than 70 Recipes for Enjoying
Nature's Most Delicious Superfood

LARA FERRONI

SASQUATCH BOOKS
SEATTLE

contents

introduction

I'll be honest: avocados and I do not go way back. In fact, barring the dreaded lima bean (still on my list of most feared foods), the mashed-up green goop was probably my most disliked food as a kid. I may have memories of my older brother torturing me with a wretched browning slice when I was younger, but that could have just been a nightmare. That's how much I used to dread them. But somewhere along the way something changed, as things do as you get a little older and a little wiser. I realized that maybe there was something to this whole avocado thing. Maybe all avocados don't taste like rotten green bacon. Maybe I had just never had a good avocado. Maybe a perfectly ripe avocado with a little salt, an olive oil drizzle, and a spoon is exactly what I want for lunch almost every day. Or in the morning with my eggs. Or at dinner in my salad. Or even in my dessert. Maybe you'll see a little smile on my face when I see that five-for-three-dollars deal in the produce section. Maybe a few will make their way into my shopping basket as an indulgence, even though they aren't. Maybe I've found that they are on my list of top ten foods, one of the few I can't imagine giving up. As it turns out, I'm not only an avocado convert . . . I'm an avocado evangelist!

And that's a good thing, because avocados really are a superfood. Avocados are packed with nutrients (about twenty vitamins and minerals) and healthy fats that help keep you energized throughout the day. Avocados also act as nutrient boosters, so adding a little avocado to your greens helps your body absorb even more of their good stuff. In fact, adding an avocado a day to a healthy diet has been shown to reduce the risk of heart disease, improve LDL cholesterol levels, and lower levels of oxidative stress in the bloodstream when eaten after other foods. In one study by the National Health and Nutrition Examination Survey (NHANES) from 2001 to 2008, participants who had enjoyed an avocado in the previous twenty-four hours were found to have greater fiber, potassium, vitamin K, and vitamin E absorption than adults who consumed no avocado. Avocados have more potassium than bananas. An average-size avocado has four grams of protein and contains eighteen of the important amino acids needed for the body's protein-building processes. The vitamin C, vitamin E, and carotenoid antioxidants found in avocados have been shown to improve skin tone.

Not to mention, some studies have shown that avocados are one of the best foods for managing your waistline. The good fats, proteins, and fiber in an avocado help fill you up and keep you full longer. Several studies have shown that a diet rich in monounsaturated fat may actually prevent body fat distribution around the belly by regulating the expression of certain fat genes, and others show that the fat in avocados helps boost your metabolism, letting you get more out of your workouts.

It's easy to work an avocado into your daily diet. Cooking with avocados goes way beyond game-time guacamole! Their smooth, buttery flavor is subtle enough to work with savory and sweet ingredients, in any meal of the day. Avocados make vegan dishes velvety and paleo recipes more satisfying. I've come up with more than seventy recipes to help you make the most of your avocados, whether you are a longtime avocado devotee or find yourself with a more recent avocado crush. I hope you enjoy!

how i cook

"I wonder if" is one of my favorite phrases, and there is always some experiment happening in my kitchen. Yeah, I'm that person who has made my own nut milk. I've even made my own version of Cheetos. There's a rumor that I may dehydrate things.

And avocados turn me into a complete avocadork. Although I'm an omnivore, I'm fascinated by whole-food, plant-based cooking when it makes the food taste amazing, and avocados make that so very easy.

Avocados can play so many roles, acting as butter in baked goods, cream in dressings or smoothies, or even eggs in homemade mayo. Avocado can take the lead in sandwiches, or play a supporting character adding richness to your salads and sides.

So throughout this book, you'll see recipes that are vegan (or could easily be made vegan) right next to those that are definitively carnivorous. I let flavor be my judge. If I don't think there's a good plant-based substitute, I won't make the suggestion. And if I think the substitute is even better than the original (like in the Avocado Ginger Latte, page 28), I'll write the recipe that way.

While experimental, the food I cook is pretty simple, and I aim for (although don't always manage) an eclectic but streamlined pantry. You'll find that many of the recipes in this book use a similar set of seasonings, so if you buy an ingredient for one recipe, you'll probably be able to use it again in another. This is especially important for the few ingredients that may be hard to find. If you have had to order a can of sweetened condensed coconut milk on Amazon.com (you can, by the way), you'll want to be sure to use all of it. As much as possible, I've tried to suggest great ways to use any extra ingredients, so there's minimal waste. For example, many recipes call for just part of an avocado—the rest can be popped into the freezer and used the next day in a smoothie.

avocado basics

ON EATING AN AVOCADO A DAY

This is not one of those miracle cookbooks in which I promise you that eating an avocado every day is going to make you magically lose ten pounds, give you glowing skin, make your hair unbreakable, or miraculously solve any of your health problems. That's not what this book is about. I love avocados for a simpler reason: they are an amazing versatile fruit that make things delicious.

Sure, even moderate consumption of the monounsaturated fat oleic acid found in avocados has been reported to both increase satiety (meaning you happily eat less), while at the same time boosting metabolism and helping you burn more calories. I know if I start my morning with a hunk of avocado, I hardly notice when lunchtime rolls around, and it does feel easier for me to motivate myself to get off the couch and get moving. But while eating my Green Power Oatmeal (page 36) in the morning may help me drop a pound or two, I'll happily put it right back on when I slurp down a boozy Cado-Rita (page 172) on Saturday night.

Avocado is rich in vitamins, minerals, and phytonutrients, as well as having natural antibacterial and antifungal properties, all of which can be good for your skin and hair, whether you rub it on directly or add it to your diet. With all the avocado recipe testing I've been doing, my skin must be positively radioactive by now.

And, in addition to their nutritional contribution, foods made with avocado have been shown to provide health benefits like lowering cholesterol and helping to prevent cancer. These are all great things. But since I'm not a research scientist, nutritionist, or doctor, I hold a certain amount of skepticism for both scientific studies and folklore remedies I find. So I like to stick with the one thing no one can dispute: avocados are delicious. And I make some fantastic dishes with them!

That's not to say that you should eat your weight in avocados. Moderation, of course, is important. If you are on a fat-restricted diet, you should be aware that an average avocado has about twenty-two grams of fat. The USDA recommends you consume between forty-four and seventy grams of fat in a day, so a whole avocado eats up a substantial part for your daily intake. If you eat an avocado everyday, it's best to use most of it as a replacement for other fats you might consume, instead of adding it to an already fat-rich diet. Many of the recipes in this book use avocado as a more nutritious replacement for oils and butter.

Also, are you allergic to latex? Then make sure you talk with your doctor before indulging in avocados. People with serious latex allergies often respond with symptoms after eating avocados.

HOW TO BUY AN AVOCADO

Avocados ripen off the tree, so don't worry if they're a little firm when you buy them. In fact, it's best to buy them a little underripe, unless you need to cook with them the same day.

To check out whether an avocado is the perfect ripeness for eating fresh, check the stem. Use your index finger to slightly push down on the stem. If the stem strongly resists, the avocado isn't quite ripe. If it sinks in too easily, it's overripe. It should give just a little resistance.

You can also lightly pull on the stem, to check the ripeness. If the stem nub doesn't come off easily, the avocado is not quite ripe yet. If it comes off easily and is light white-green underneath the stem, the avocado is just right. If it's brown under the stem (or the stem is missing and looks dry and brown), the avocado may be overripe.

You should also carefully cradle the avocado in the palm of your hand and very gently squeeze to make sure there are no hollow spots under the peel.

Unless specified, "an avocado" in this book refers to an average medium Hass avocado, since that's what you'll mostly likely find at your store. This avocado will be approximately a half pound (eight ounces) when it's whole. A small avocado is typically about five to six ounces, and large avocados can vary from almost one pound to even larger.

Depending on your avocado variety, your mileage may vary, but as a general rule, you'll get about one cup of avocado for every medium avocado.

are avocados always in season?

Yes and no.

A trip to the grocery store may make you think that every avocado is a Hass, and that they are in season year-round. That's probably because over 90 percent of the avocados on shop shelves are Hass, which ship and store especially well and have a great flavor and mouthfeel to boot.

The first Hass avocado was grown in the early 1920s by A. R. Rideout in La Habra Heights, California. He sold the seedling to the fruit's namesake, Rudolph Hass, who patented the fruit in 1935. That original tree produced fruit for eighty years and was the origin of millions of avocado trees.

HASS AVOCADOS grow nearly year-round in Mexico and have a very long growing season in California. Their purple-black pebbled peel is what most of us think about as a ripe avocado. But despite their evergreen appearance on store shelves, Hass avocados are seasonal, and an avocado will always taste its best in season. California Hass avocados are best from April to September. Due to a wide variety of climate zones in Mexico's main avocado growing region, Michoacán, Mexico's avocados are available almost all year-round, but they are best from August to April. So, when you are buying Hass avocados, be sure to check the origin, and buy in season for the best flavor.

But the world of avocados goes beyond Hass. Would it surprise you to find out that there are over nine hundred varieties of avocados, about twenty of them grown commercially in the United States? These varieties are well worth seeking out when they are available.

FUERTE AVOCADOS are the second most common variety found in most grocery stores, after Hass. These slightly elongated pear-shaped avocados have a thin green peel, even when ripe. If you bought avocados in the 1950s, they probably would have been Fuertes. While their peel is thin, they're relatively easy to peel, and their flesh is light but not watery. I got my Fuertes from Rancho Charanda Citrus Ranch via LocalHarvest.org.

BACON AVOCADOS are related to Fuertes (and Zutanos), and they don't actually taste like bacon. In fact, when ripe, they are slightly sweet. Like other Guatemalan-strain varieties, these avocados can be lower in fat and a little higher in water content, which makes them better in smoothies or recipes that aren't using the avocado as a butter replacement. I got my Bacon avocados, which were beautiful and delicious, from the fine folks at Friend's Ranch (FriendsRanches.com) at the tail end of their short season, December to February. They also grow and ship Fuertes and Hass.

CHOQUETTE (OR FLORIDA) AVOCADOS, grown unsurprisingly in Florida, are one of the largest avocados and have a shiny green peel, even when ripe, resembling a mango. These avocados tend to be a little lower in fat and have a fruity, slightly grassy flavor. While you can make guacamole with these avocados, I recommend making the Thin Guacamole (page 50) from them because traditional thick guacamole with less fat just isn't as luscious. Choquette season is October through December, although I was able to get some in late January from Fresh Gardens on LocalHarvest.org.

Big Hass

Fuerte

Choquette

Little Hass

MEXICOLA GRANDE AVOCADOS are a rare breed with an almost paper-thin peel that is edible. Technically, all avocado peel is edible, but it's definitely not palatable. These shiny black avocados resemble small eggplants, and are available August through January.

LAMB HASS AVOCADOS may begin to give standard Hass avocados a run for their money. With the same thick peel that turns black when ripe and a similar fat content as Hass, Lamb Hass are buttery and nutty in flavor, perfect for fresh guacamole. They tend to be a bit larger and, for farmers, even more tolerant to winds and high temperatures than Hass. Lamb Hass mature in the summer, so look for them June through August.

REED AVOCADOS can be harder to find in the United States, but they are reasonably common in Australia and New Zealand. With a similar fat content to Hass, these avocados are on the larger side, and they are beautifully buttery. Their almost golden flesh is perfect for a quick spread on toast or sliced on a salad in the fall. While Reed avocados have thicker peels like Hass, they don't turn black, so if they give a little when you apply light pressure, they are ripe.

SHARWIL AVOCADOS are one of the stars of Hawaii's commercial avocados. Originally from Australia and highly regarded there, Sharwils have a high fat content that is on par with Hass, but the Sharwil typically has a smaller pit, meaning more creamy flesh to indulge in. Hawaiian-grown Sharwils are available from late November through April. Imports of Hawaiian avocados to the US mainland stopped in 1992 due to problems with fruit flies, but in 2013 the USDA reversed the ban; you may now see Sharwils on supermarket shelves in the winter when California avocados are scarce. You might also find them at local farmers' markets if you live in Southern California. I've seen them at Santa Monica's farmers' markets on occasion.

SHEPARD AVOCADOS are another variety found mostly in Australia. They are similar to Fuerte varieties in size, shape, and color. The fruit of this avocado is nutty and rich, with a slightly gluey texture. Unlike most avocado varieties, Shepards tend not to brown once cut. Because of that, it's a great variety to use on any to-go foods like sandwiches or salads, but because they get a little sticky when mashed, they aren't recommended for guacamole. In the United States, you'll find them August through October.

ZUTANO AVOCADOS, like Fuertes, are slightly pear shaped, with a very smooth, thin green peel. Their fruit is light and creamy, and they work well on salads or in baking. Zutanos would be great in Thin Guacamole (page 50), but stick with a fattier avocado for Thick Guacamole (page 50). Zutanos are in season in the winter in California.

are avocados eco-friendly?

You may not live in a location that makes it easy for you to grow your own fruit-bearing avocado tree (although you can certainly try; see page 16), so your avocados are going to have to travel a ways to get to you. How do you make sure you get the most eco-friendly avocado possible?

The good news is that avocado trees are generally considered sustainable. A mature tree can crank out between one hundred and four hundred avocados a year on fruiting years (some varieties only produce every two or three years) and provides a rich eco-canopy that supports birds and honeybees. Avocado trees are significant water consumers, but they have a relatively low impact compared to most other commercially grown crops.

There are plenty of organic avocado choices available, and since avocados are peeled before consumption, you don't have to worry about choosing avocados grown with pesticides.

To get the most eco-friendly avocado, look for avocados that are in season, ideally at your local farmers' market, or on seasonal produce sites that work directly with farmers, like LocalHarvest.org.

HOW TO STORE AN AVOCADO

You can store unripe avocados at room temperature for up to a few days. When an avocado is ripe, you can slow the aging by storing it in the refrigerator for a day or two.

Once cut, you are fighting a battle between oxidation and the avocado's beautiful green flesh. It's a myth that leaving the pit in the avocado will prevent it from browning (at least anywhere that isn't covered by the pit). The trick is to keep air off of the avocado flesh as much as possible, so it's better to remove the pit, brush it with a little bit of avocado (or olive) oil, and wrap it tightly with plastic wrap, or use one of those nifty avocado keepers that have a bump for the pit hole to create a complete seal on the half of an avocado (you can find them in specialty kitchen shops or on Amazon.com). Lemon or lime juice brushed on the avocado flesh can also help slow the browning process.

There's also a rumor that storing an avocado in an airtight container with a slice of onion or a peeled clove of garlic helps keep the brown away, due to the sulfur compounds that get released. In my tests I saw no improvement to the avocado when stored with onion, so I recommend sticking with simply wrapping the avocado as tightly as possible to keep the air off of the surface.

HOW TO FREEZE AN AVOCADO

You can also freeze avocados to use in smoothies, sauces, or baked goods. (Throughout the book, I've noted whether a recipe works well with frozen avocados!) To freeze an avocado, slice it into cubes, and then place the pieces in a single layer on a waxed paper–lined baking sheet that will fit in your freezer. Freeze the avocado cubes until they're solid, about thirty

minutes, and then transfer them to an airtight container that you keep in the freezer. To defrost, place the cubes you need in a bowl of water until thawed, five to ten minutes, and then drain. Unless specified, you should defrost any frozen avocado.

HOW TO CUT AN AVOCADO

The best way to slice an avocado is to make a careful cut lengthwise from stem to end, letting your sharp knife roll around the pit. Gently rotate the two halves (still connected by the pit) to separate. Use a chef's knife to carefully whack the pit, which will wedge the pit on the blade. Then give a little twist, and the pit will easily pull out.

To keep the half avocado intact, make a small cut just below the stem and then gently pull the peel away, similar to how you'd peel a banana. This is called the "nick and peel" approach.

To make slices, you can use the "nick and peel" approach or leave the avocado in the peel, and gently slice through the avocado flesh with horizontal strokes using just the tip of the knife. Try not to pierce the peel (but don't worry if you do). Then, pull away the peel, starting at one end to release the slices.

To make cubes, slice the avocado in the peel as you would if you were making slices, but slice both horizontally and vertically. Use a spoon to gently pull back the peel and scoop out the avocado cubes. Do try to get as close to the peel as possible, as that's where most of the phytonutrients are!

For avocados with thinner peels, it may be easier to peel the avocado once it has been cut in half before slicing or cubing.

HOW TO HEAT AN AVOCADO

You'll notice that only a few recipes in this book instruct you to cook the avocados, either in relatively small amounts as a butter substitute or cooked for a very short time in a soup, under the broiler, or tossed into a skillet at the last minute. The reason for this is simple: when some avocados are cooked through, they get decidedly bitter. You may not notice it at first, but there's a distinctive bitter, almost musky, aftertaste that lingers, even an hour after you've indulged. Trust me on this one . . . you don't want to eat a well-cooked avocado.

That's one of the reasons you won't see a recipe in this book for an egg cooked in the hollow of a cut avocado—the time it takes for the egg to cook is much too long for the avocado to hold up to the heat. Bitterness is very likely to ensue.

If you want warm avocado, stick to recipes that either have a very short cooking time, or add the avocado just at the end.

HOW TO GROW YOUR OWN AVOCADO PLANT

If you eat a lot of avocados, you'll end up with a lot of avocado pits. Sure, you can just compost them. (Or, if you are curious, you can eat them! See page 22.) But why not try a little science experiment and see if you can grow your own tree? If you are living in a warm climate, grow a couple of trees and wait quite a few more years, and you might even get fruit. (If you are keeping your tree indoors, you're probably out of luck on that front.)

Starting your plant is easy. Just take a clean avocado pit and poke three toothpicks into it evenly spaced around the equator of the pit. Place the pit, pointy side up, over a jar of water so that the toothpicks hold it in

place and a half inch or so of water covers the bottom of the pit. Place the jar in a warm spot, out of direct sunlight, and change the water at least once a week, topping off with more water during the week as needed. Most pits will start sprouting roots within two to three weeks, but some may take up to eight weeks. If you don't see any roots by then, your pit is probably a dud.

Once you see roots, you'll shortly see a stem coming out of the top. When the stem is six to seven inches long, cut it back to about three inches, and then continue to let it grow a few more weeks, until it has leaves again. Now it's ready to plant!

To plant, fill a ten-inch pot with rich soil. Create a well in the center of the soil, place the pit in the well with the roots down, and cover the roots with more soil, leaving about half of the pit uncovered. Water when the soil gets dry, but don't overdo it. If your avocado leaves start to yellow, you are overwatering.

Did you know there's a whole community out there on growing avocados at home? Check out Facebook.com/Groups/AvocadoSociety for answers to your avocado growing questions.

OTHER AVOCADO INGREDIENTS

avocado butter

Avocado butter may sound like a fascinating nut butter replacement, but alas, there isn't any food-grade avocado butter available to cook with. On the plus side, avocado is a great moisturizer for your skin, especially post-sun. It melts easily and goes on silk smooth. Avocado butter is available on Amazon.com or from DIY soap-making supply companies like BrambleBerry.com.

> Try it in a lip balm! Just place **¼ cup avocado butter** in a microwave-safe bowl, along with **¼ cup beeswax** (available in craft stores) and microwave in 30-second intervals until melted. If you want to add some flavor or scent, stir about **½ teaspoon of an extract or essential oil** into the melted oils (try peppermint!). Pour the mixture into sterilized containers of your choice (like small slide-top or round tins) and allow them to cool completely before using.

avocado honey

Avocado honey comes from bees that hang out in avocado groves. It's a win-win situation, because the trees need the bees to pollinate, and the honey the bees produce is not your average table honey. It's dark and a little spicy with hints of molasses and butter. I highly recommend it in any of the recipes in this book that call for honey. It may be hard to find avocado honey in your local market, but LocalHarvest.org has seasonal avocado honey from small farms available online.

avocado leaf

Avocado leaves, often found at Latin American grocers (but also available on Amazon.com or off your own tree if you are growing your own!), have a subtle anise flavor, similar to fennel pollen, and are often used as a seasoning in Central American cooking. I highly recommend the Avocado Leaf Salt (page 71) or sticking a few leaves in a small jar of sugar for a subtle licorice-scented sugar.

avocado oil

Avocado oil has a similar nutty quality as olive oil but with a slightly more grassy bite. It's fantastic whisked into salad dressings or drizzled over grilled meats as a finishing oil, and with a smoke point of 520 degrees F (270 degrees C), one of the highest of plant-based oils, it's also ideal for sautéing and frying. Although not required, I highly recommend avocado oil in any of the recipes in this book that call for oil.

Avocado oil also makes a great conditioning treatment for your hair. Just massage a quarter-size dollop of oil into your scalp and through to the ends, and then rinse.

You can find avocado oil at specialty markets. La Tourangelle make unrefined avocado oil that is great for salads (but I don't recommend it for higher temperatures). Spectrum Naturals and Chosen Foods make delicious (although less flavorful) refined avocado oils that are good as a finishing oil or for high-heat uses.

avocado pit

Avocado pits are in fact edible and, as it turns out, very nutritious: 70 percent of an avocado's antioxidants are in the pit. However, they taste terribly bitter, so I'm not recommending eating one. If you do want to try it out, though, here's what you do:

Cut the avocado pit in half with a very sharp knife, lay it flat side down, and cut each half into a few smaller pieces. Puree the pit in a high-powered blender and pulse until you have a moist powder, scraping down the sides as needed. Let the powder dry completely at room temperature and then store it in an airtight container. You can then add a bit of this powder to your smoothies, baked goods, or sauces. But, be warned, the powder is very bitter and a little goes a long way.

OTHER SPECIALTY INGREDIENTS

Most of the recipes in this book can be made with ingredients found in your typical grocery store, but there are a few specialty ingredients that I think are worth seeking out.

Sweetened condensed coconut milk pairs so beautifully with avocado, I use it in quite a few recipes in place of traditional sweetened condensed milk. While you can certainly use the dairy version, if you can find the coconut version (or are inclined to order on Amazon.com), I think you'll be hooked as much as I am. I like Nature's Charm brand.

I like to use almond milk in many recipes, but I always use the unsweetened original flavor. Be sure not to substitute in vanilla flavored or any sweetened variety! If possible, make your own nut milk (like the Cashew Milk, page 128), and avoid any of the fillers and preservatives. Or feel free to substitute in any unsweetened milk of your choice (dairy, nut, or otherwise).

TOOLS

A high-powered blender, like a Vitamix, makes easy work out of pureeing avocado without having to stop and scrape down the sides repeatedly. In addition, avocado pureed with a blender gets aerated and thickens more easily than other ways of pureeing, such as a food processor. This is perfect for smoothies and soups but also for making the crème brûlée base on page 157 or in the chocolate frosting on page 158. I had much better luck with the blender than I did with either a food processor or a mixer with a whisk attachment in both of those recipes.

breakfast

GREEN SMOOTHIE

If you aren't adding avocado to your green juice, you are missing out. Not only will the avocado make your juice into a delicious dairy-free smoothie, the avocado will help you get more nutrition from any leafy greens in the juice.

MAKES 2 SERVINGS

1 medium apple, cored and cut into quarters

½ avocado, frozen (see page 13)

1 cup packed baby spinach, baby kale, or a combination

¼ cup fresh mint

½ cup coconut water or cold water

¼ cup freshly squeezed lime juice (from about 2 small limes)

Pinch of kosher salt

6 to 7 ice cubes

• In a high-powered blender, place all of the ingredients and pulse until thick. Serve immediately.

AVOCADO GINGER LATTE

Cozy slippers, a warm fire, and this frothy, spiced latte equal
the perfect fall morning.

MAKES 1 SERVING

1 cup unsweetened
   almond milk or milk
   of choice
1 tablespoon avocado
   honey
1 tablespoon
   smashed avocado,
   fresh or frozen
   and defrosted
   (see page 13)

1 teaspoon peeled
   and chopped
   fresh ginger
Pinch of kosher salt

• In a heavy-bottomed pan over medium-low heat, heat the almond milk until it simmers at about 160 degrees F and is a little steamy, then remove it from the heat.

• In a high-powered blender, place the honey, avocado, ginger, and salt. Pour the warmed milk into the blender and then pulse until the mixture is smooth and frothy. Serve immediately.

• Bonus points: Add 1 teaspoon of peeled and chopped fresh turmeric to boost the anti-inflammatory properties of this drink!

GREEN EGGS

I would eat these on a boat, and I would eat these with a goat. I would eat these here or there. I would eat these anywhere.

MAKES 1 SERVING

¼ cup smashed
avocado

2 tablespoons crème
fraîche, sour cream,
or yogurt

2 large eggs

½ teaspoon kosher
salt

2 teaspoons avocado
oil or unsalted
butter

- In a small bowl, use a fork to blend the avocado and crème fraîche. Don't worry if it's not completely smooth. Some chunks are good. Set aside.

- In a medium bowl, place the eggs and salt. Using an immersion blender, blend the mixture until smooth, less than 1 minutes. Set aside.

- In a heavy-bottomed skillet over medium-low heat, add the avocado oil and then pour in the blended eggs. Using a rubber spatula, stir the mixture until the eggs thicken but are still a little wet, 2 to 4 minutes. Remove the skillet from the heat, fold in the avocado mixture, and let it sit for another 30 seconds before serving.

BLUEBERRY & AVOCADO MUFFINS

A little avocado gives these muffins a fantastic tender and moist crumb and the perfect crust. I suggest making a double batch and freezing any you don't gobble up immediately. Reheated in a 350-degree-F oven for eight minutes or microwaved for thirty seconds, they make a perfect morning snack.

MAKES 1 DOZEN MUFFINS

1½ cups plus 2 tablespoons unbleached all-purpose flour, divided

⅓ cup sugar

2 teaspoons baking powder

½ teaspoon kosher salt

½ cup avocado, fresh or frozen and defrosted (see page 13), mashed

1 large egg, beaten

⅓ cup warm water

2 tablespoons coconut oil, melted

1 heaping cup fresh or frozen blueberries

• Preheat oven to 400 degrees F. Line a muffin tin with muffin liners or lightly grease it with coconut oil.

• In a large bowl, sift together 1½ cups of the flour, the sugar, baking powder, and salt. Set aside.

• In an small bowl, combine the avocado, egg, water, oil and beat it with a fork until combined. Add the egg mixture to the flour mixture, and mix until just combined (do not overmix).

• In a small bowl, place the remaining 2 tablespoons flour, and stir in the blueberries to coat them with flour, then toss them into the batter and give it a light stir.

• Scoop the batter into the muffin cups, and bake until the muffins are golden brown, about 20 minutes. Let the muffins cool for 5 minutes before removing them from the muffin tin.

AVOCADO WAFFLES

This plant-based, vegan waffle recipe started out as a pancake recipe. After repeated attempts of pancakes with a delightfully crisp crust but too moist interior, I finally realized their true nature.

MAKES 3 TO 4 WAFFLES

1 cup unbleached all-purpose flour

1 tablespoon sugar

2 teaspoons baking powder

½ teaspoon kosher salt

1 cup unsweetened almond milk or milk of choice

⅓ cup smashed avocado, fresh or frozen and defrosted (see page 13)

¼ cup water

1 tablespoon melted coconut oil, plus more for cooking

1 teaspoon apple cider vinegar

1 teaspoon vanilla extract

Syrup, fruit, nuts, or honey, for serving (optional)

• In a large bowl, whisk together the flour, sugar, baking powder, and salt, and then form a well in the center.

• In a medium or large bowl, mix the almond milk, avocado, water, oil, vinegar, and vanilla until smooth. Pour the milk mixture into the well in the flour mixture, and stir with a fork until just mixed. Lumps are OK, but try to get all the dry ingredients on the sides and bottom moistened.

• Heat your waffle iron at its highest setting, and brush it lightly with coconut oil. Pour about ⅓ cup of the batter onto the iron, and follow your manufacturer's instructions for cooking, likely about 3 minutes. Take care opening the waffle iron; if it doesn't want to open, let it cook a little longer.

• Serve immediately with the toppings of your choice, or keep the waffles in a warm oven until ready to serve. Waffles can be reheated in the toaster later.

AVOCADO YOGURT

Avocado makes a great upgrade to your daily sweet or savory yogurt. You'll be shocked at how silky your yogurt becomes! For savory yogurt, try topping it with salted pepitas, sunflower seeds, microgreens, or even as a dollop on unsweetened porridge. For sweet yogurt, try topping it with your favorite jam or fruit, or mix in a little cinnamon to taste.

MAKES 1 SERVING

⅓ cup Greek yogurt of choice

⅓ cup smashed avocado, fresh or frozen and defrosted (see page 13)

For savory yogurt:
Pinch of sea salt
1 teaspoon freshly squeezed lime juice

For sweet yogurt:
2 tablespoons honey
1 tablespoon freshly squeezed lemon juice

• In a blender, place the yogurt and avocado. For savory yogurt, add the salt and lime juice; for sweet yogurt, add the honey and lemon juice. Puree until smooth.

• Avocado yogurt is best eaten immediately, but it will keep its color in an airtight container in the refrigerator for a couple of days. It will gradually fade to gray, but it will still taste OK for a couple of additional days.

GREEN POWER OATMEAL

Now, this is the way to start your day. Savory, nubby steel-cut oats boosted with a whole lot of superfoods, this bowlful has a great balance between carbs and proteins to fill you up and keep you going all morning long. Want to amp up the protein even more? Add a poached or fried egg on top.

MAKES 2 SERVINGS

2 cups plus 2 tablespoons water

Kosher salt

½ cup steel-cut oats

1 tablespoon flaxseeds

1 tablespoon chia seeds

1 small avocado, half mashed (about ½ cup), half sliced, divided

2 to 3 tablespoons freshly squeezed lemon juice, divided

¼ cup unsweetened yogurt

1 tablespoon lemon zest

2 teaspoons avocado oil, divided

2 teaspoons chives, finely chopped, divided

1 cup baby arugula or other baby greens

¼ cup slivered almonds or chopped toasted hazelnuts

Pinch flaky sea salt

Freshly crushed black pepper

• In a medium pot over high heat, bring 2 cups of the water to a boil with a pinch of salt. Reduce the heat to low, add the oats, and simmer for 20 minutes. Add the flaxseeds and chia seeds, and simmer until most of the water has been absorbed, about 10 minutes more.

• While the oats are cooking, in a medium bowl, place the mashed avocado and about 1 tablespoon of the lemon juice and stir to combine. Add the yogurt, lemon zest, the remaining 1 to 2 tablespoons lemon juice, 1 teaspoon of the avocado oil, 1 teaspoon of the chives, the remaining 2 tablespoons water, and a pinch of salt. If the mixture is too thick to drizzle, you can add a bit more water to achieve the desired thickness. It should be about the thickness of ranch dressing.

• Split the oats between two bowls, and stir in the remaining 1 teaspoon avocado oil. Top with the avocado slices, arugula, and nuts. Drizzle with the avocado-yogurt sauce, sprinkle on the remaining 1 teaspoon chives, and serve immediately.

TIP: Steel-cut oats can take a while to cook, but they can be precooked the night before, so your breakfast can come together in a snap. To precook your oats, add them to the same amount of boiling water, and simmer them for just 1 minute. Transfer the contents of the pot to a container with a cover, and refrigerate overnight. In the morning, just transfer all of the contents back into a pot over low heat, and proceed with the directions on the opposite, starting with adding the flaxseeds and chia seeds.

TROPICAL POWER OATMEAL

If you usually eat sugary oat porridge, this one may take a little getting used to, since it relies only on the fruit for its subtle, tangy sweetness. I find it refreshing, but feel free to stir in a spoonful of brown sugar to the oats if you need a little more.

MAKES 4 SERVINGS

4 cups water

1 cup steel-cut oats

2 tablespoons flax-seeds (optional)

2 tablespoons chia seeds (optional)

1 small avocado, sliced into 1-inch cubes

1 small mango, sliced into 1-inch cubes

½ cup fresh pineapple chunks

2 tablespoons freshly squeezed lime juice, divided

2 teaspoons lime zest, divided

½ teaspoon kosher salt

2 to 3 tablespoons sweet Avocado Yogurt (optional) (page 35)

¼ cup unsweetened coconut flakes

- In a medium pot over high heat, bring the water to a boil with a pinch of salt. Reduce the heat to low, add the oats, and simmer for 20 minutes more. Add the flaxseeds and chia seeds, and simmer until most of the water has been absorbed, about 10 minutes more.

- In a small bowl, place the avocado, mango, pineapple chunks, 1 tablespoon of the lime juice, and 1 teaspoon of the lime zest. Give it a gentle stir to coat. Set aside.

- When the oats are ready, stir in the salt and the remaining 1 tablespoon lime juice and 1 teaspoon lime zest. Split the oats between four bowls, top them with the fruit mixture and yogurt, sprinkle them with the coconut flakes, and serve.

NOTE: These oats are also great served as a cold treat. Make the oats in the evening, chill overnight, then top them with the fruit and take them on the go.

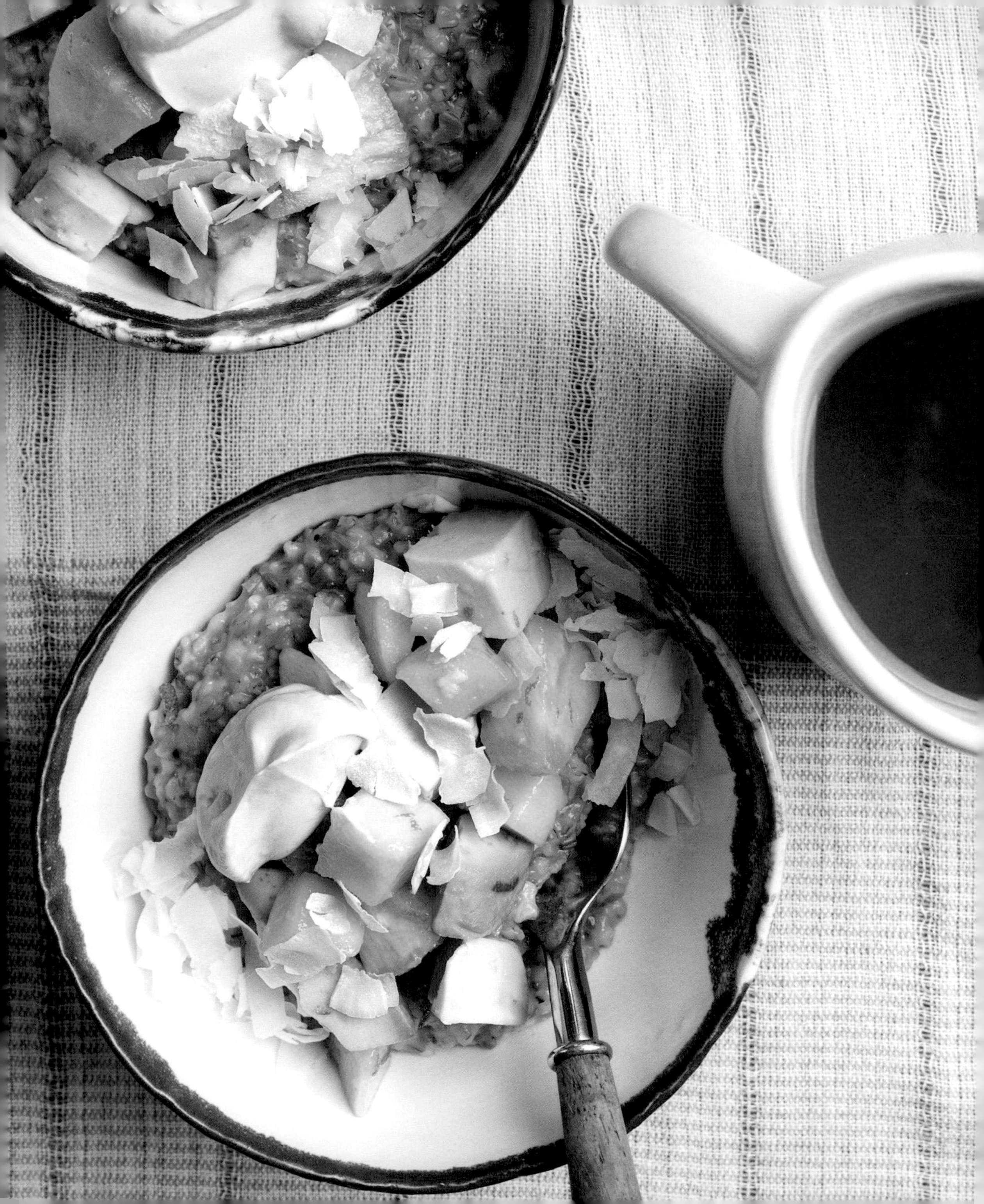

AVOCADO GRITS & GREENS

Here's to learning to love foods you used to hate. This dish hits all of my childhood food phobias—grits, greens, and avocados—but now it's one of my favorites.

MAKES 2 TO 4 SERVINGS

1 cup yellow or white corn grits (not instant)

1 bunch kale or chard

1 tablespoon avocado oil or canola oil

1 teaspoon crushed garlic

2 teaspoons soy sauce

¼ cup smashed avocado, fresh or frozen and defrosted (see page 13)

2 tablespoons chopped roasted nuts (optional)

Avocado slices (optional)

- Prepare the grits according the package's directions.

- While the grits are cooking, remove the stems from the kale, and cut the rest of the leaves into ribbons.

- In a medium skillet over medium-high heat, add the oil. When hot, add the kale and garlic. Sauté until wilted, 3 to 4 minutes, and then remove the skillet from the heat. Stir in the soy sauce.

- When the grits are soft and creamy, stir in the smashed avocado. Divide the grits between two to four bowls, and top each serving with the greens and the nuts and avocado slices, if using. Serve immediately.

AVOCADO TOAST

step 1: make toast

step 2: top it with avocado and other yummy stuff

step 3: eat

Sourdough,
smashed avocado,
cucumber, chili
flake, fish sauce

Sourdough,
smashed avocado,
nectarine slices,
fresh mozzarella,
fresh mint

Sourdough, sliced
avocado,
strawberries,
balsamic vinegar

Sourdough, diced
avocado, bacon
jam, arugula

Brioche loaf,
smashed avocado,
banana, cinnamon,
sugar

Brioche loaf,
sliced avocado,
scrambled egg,
hot sauce

Brioche loaf, sliced
avocado, Nutella,
pear slices

Brioche loaf,
smashed avocado,
mandarin orange
segments, coconut
cream, fresh mint

Baguette, sliced
avocado, almond
butter, honey,
lemon juice

Baguette,
smashed avocado,
radish slices, Herbs
de Provence,
flakey sea salt

Baguette,
smashed avocado,
grilled romaine,
boquerónes

Baguette,
sliced avocado,
marmalade,
flakey sea salt

Bagel, smashed
avocado, summer
tomato slices,
fresh basil

Bagel, diced
avocado, pickled
beets, chèvre

Bagel, sliced
avocado, smashed
sweet potato,
ricotta salata

Bagel, smashed
avocado, feta,
black sesame
seeds, cilantro,
lime juice

Lettuce, smashed avocado, apple slices, cabbage, poppy-seed dressing

Pita, diced avocado, roasted poblano (or jala-peño), crema

Chip, sliced avocado, cheddar, caramelized onions

Cracker, smashed avocado, pepper jelly

dips, spreads & condiments

Thick Guacamole 50

Thin Guacamole 50

Creamy Guacamole 51

Spicy Guacamole 51

Chunky Guacamole 57

Avocado Mayo 59

Avocado Pickles 60

Avocado Chutney 63

Avocado Kimchi 64

Avocado Green Goddess Dressing 66

Avocado Ranch Dressing 68

Avocado Poppy-Seed Dressing 69

Avocado Compound Butter 70

Avocado Leaf Salt 71

THICK GUACAMOLE

Avocados at their prime? This is the guac for you. Resist the temptation to overseason, and let the avocado's own flavor shine. Instead of chips, try serving with cucumber slices.

MAKES ABOUT 1 CUP GUACAMOLE

1 avocado

1 to 2 teaspoons seeded and minced serrano pepper

½ teaspoon freshly squeezed lime juice

¼ teaspoon sea salt

Pinch of lime zest

• In a medium bowl, put all of the ingredients. Mash the ingredients with the back of a spoon until just combined and the avocado is well mashed with some chunks, and serve immediately.

THIN GUACAMOLE

In Oaxaca guacamole is traditionally a thinner sauce, perfect for drizzling on carne asada or your favorite tacos. It's also delicious on chips.

MAKES ABOUT 1 CUP GUACAMOLE

1 avocado, fresh or frozen and defrosted (see page 13)

½ medium jalapeño, seeded and chopped

1 tablespoon freshly squeezed lime juice

1 teaspoon lime zest

½ teaspoon crushed garlic

¼ to ½ cup water

Sea salt

• In the bowl of a food processor, place the avocado, jalapeño, lime juice and zest, and garlic. Pulse once or twice to combine. Add ¼ cup of the water, and continue to pulse until smooth. Add a bit more water, if needed, to keep the blades moving. When the guacamole is smooth, add salt to taste. Serve immediately or cover well and refrigerate; this guacamole keeps reasonably well in the refrigerator for 24 hours.

CREAMY GUACAMOLE

Just a little ricotta blended into this guac makes it unbelievably creamy and perfect for spreading onto your favorite bagel or toast.

MAKES ABOUT 1 CUP GUACAMOLE

1 fresh avocado
2 tablespoons ricotta
2 teaspoons freshly
   squeezed lime juice

½ teaspoon lime zest
½ teaspoon sea salt

- In a medium bowl, put all of the ingredients. Mash the ingredients with the back of a spoon until just combined, and serve immediately or cover well and refrigerate for up to a couple of hours.

SPICY GUACAMOLE

Like it hot? This one is smokin'. Need more heat? Substitute a habanero for the jalapeño.

MAKES ABOUT 1 CUP GUACAMOLE

1 fresh avocado
1 jalapeño, chopped
1 tablespoon freshly
   squeezed lime juice
1 teaspoon lime zest

¼ teaspoon sea salt
¼ teaspoon cayenne
   pepper
Pinch of smoked hot
   paprika

- In a medium bowl, put the avocado, jalapeño, lime juice and zest, salt, and cayenne pepper. Mash the ingredients with the back of a spoon until just combined, garnish with the paprika, and serve immediately.

Thin Guacamole

Creamy Guacamole

Spicy Guacamole

CHUNKY GUACAMOLE

Want a little more going on in your guacamole? This Tex-Mex version blends traditional thick guacamole with pico de gallo for a hearty chip topping. It's great for nachos! Be sure to remove the seeds from the tomato and cucumber, or your guac may get watery.

MAKES ABOUT 1 CUP

2 tablespoons chopped red onion

½ small Roma tomato, seeded and finely diced

½ jalapeño, seeded and diced

2 tablespoons fresh cilantro, chopped

2 tablespoons peeled, seeded, and finely diced cucumber

1 tablespoon freshly squeezed lime juice

1 teaspoon lime zest

½ teaspoon sea salt

1 fresh avocado, diced

• In a small bowl of cold water, put the onion, and set it aside for at least 10 minutes. Drain well, and then place the onion in a separate medium bowl.

• Add the tomato, jalapeño, cilantro, cucumber, lime juice and zest, and salt to the bowl. Mix well. Stir in the avocado, folding to incorporate but leaving the avocado cubes mostly intact, and serve immediately or cover well and refrigerate for up to an hour.

AVOCADO MAYO

Make your own egg-free avocado mayo to use in any recipes requiring mayonnaise (if you aren't just using mashed avocado in place of the mayo already!).

MAKES ABOUT 1 CUP MAYO

1 cup avocado, fresh or frozen and defrosted (see page 13)

4 teaspoons freshly squeezed lemon juice

½ teaspoon Dijon mustard

⅓ cup avocado oil

Kosher salt and freshly ground pepper

- In the bowl of a food processor, put the avocado, lemon juice, and mustard and pulse to combine. With the motor running, stream in the oil, stopping to scrape down the sides occasionally. The mixture will thicken and become lighter and creamy. Add the salt and pepper to taste.

- You can store the mayo in an airtight container in the refrigerator for 2 to 3 days. The color may change a little, but the flavor should still be great.

> **TIP:** Add 1 tablespoon of rice wine vinegar to make the mayo more like **Japanese Kewpie mayo**, and mix with sriracha for a great spicy vegan mayo!
>
> ─────────────
>
> **TIP:** Make **avocado aioli** by adding ½ teaspoon crushed garlic to the mixture.

AVOCADO PICKLES

Here's a great use for your not-quite-ripe avocados. Pickling avocados softens them and makes them a perfect sandwich topping, like for the Cubano Sandwich (page 121).

MAKES 1 PINT PICKLES

½ cup distilled white or cider vinegar

½ cup water

1 tablespoon kosher salt

1 tablespoon whole yellow mustard seeds

1 teaspoon sugar

½ teaspoon black peppercorns

1 medium chile de árbol (optional)

1 or 2 very firm avocados, sliced

- In a medium nonreactive pot, whisk together the vinegar, water, salt, mustard seeds, sugar, peppercorns, and chile de árbol. Bring the mixture to a simmer over medium heat, stirring until the sugar and salt dissolve, then let it cool to room temperature, about 20 minutes.

- In a 1-pint jar, place the avocado slices, and top them with the cooled brine. Refrigerate for at least 1 hour or up to 1 month.

AVOCADO CHUTNEY

I'm a sucker for sweet-and-sour dishes, so I want to spread this chutney on everything, like the Lamb Chop with Avocado Chutney (page 142) and Spinach Avocado Phyllo Rolls (page 80). It also makes a great coleslaw dressing.

MAKES ABOUT 1 CUP CHUTNEY

¼ small red onion, chopped

¼ cup golden raisins

¼ cup sugar

2 tablespoons red wine vinegar

1 teaspoon crystallized ginger, chopped

¼ teaspoon whole yellow or brown mustard seeds

¼ teaspoon red chili flakes

½ cup finely diced avocado

- In a small skillet over medium-low heat, put the onion, raisins, sugar, vinegar, ginger, mustard seeds, and chili flakes. Cook, stirring, just until the sugar melts, about 5 minutes. Move the mixture to the bowl of a food processor, and pulse until just blended but still a little chunky. Fold in the avocado.

- Store the chutney in an airtight container in the refrigerator for up to 2 weeks.

AVOCADO KIMCHI

Be sure to use Korean chili flakes for this recipe, not the red pepper flakes you might sprinkle on a pizza. Korean chili flakes (*gochugaru*) don't have seeds and are less spicy. If you can't find green mango or green papaya, try substituting daikon or jicama.

MAKES ABOUT 2 CUPS KIMCHI

1 firm avocado, sliced into thick matchsticks

1 medium green mango or green papaya, sliced into thick matchsticks

2 green onions, trimmed and cut into 2-inch lengths

½ teaspoon sea salt

2 cloves garlic, crushed

3 tablespoons rice vinegar

2 tablespoons Korean chili flakes

1 teaspoon ginger, minced

1 teaspoon sesame oil

1 teaspoon sesame seeds

1 teaspoon sugar

• In a large bowl, put the avocado, mango, and onion, sprinkle it with the salt, and set aside.

• In a small bowl, mix the garlic, vinegar, chili flakes, ginger, oil, sesame seeds, and sugar to make a paste. Add the chili paste to the avocado mixture, and stir to coat.

• In a 1-pint jar, place the mixture, covered, and refrigerate it overnight. The kimchi will keep for up to 2 weeks, and the flavor will continue to improve over time.

AVOCADO GREEN GODDESS DRESSING

Adding fresh avocado means you can use less oil and still have a perfectly luscious dressing. Be sure to use just the leaves from the herbs, or strain it after blending. Use this dressing in slaw, on spring greens, or on veggies, like the Avocado and Artichokes (page 103).

MAKES ABOUT 1 CUP DRESSING

¾ cup smashed avocado, fresh or frozen and defrosted (see page 13)

¼ to ¾ cup water

¼ cup freshly squeezed lemon juice (from 1 large lemon)

¼ cup fresh mint

¼ cup fresh tarragon

2 tablespoons chopped fresh basil

2 tablespoons chopped chives

2 tablespoons chopped parsley

1 tablespoon lemon zest

1 tablespoon avocado oil or extra-virgin olive oil

6 anchovy fillets (optional)

1 small shallot, peeled and quartered

½ clove garlic

Kosher salt and freshly ground black pepper

• In the bowl of a food processor, put the avocado, ¼ cup of the water, lemon juice, mint, tarragon, basil, chives, parsley, lemon zest, oil, anchovy, shallot, and garlic and puree until smooth, scraping down the sides of the processor as needed. Add the remaining ½ cup water if needed to get a more pourable consistency.

• Season the dressing with the salt and pepper to taste.

• For a smoother, more restaurant-quality version, strain the dressing with a fine-mesh strainer. For a more rustic texture, leave it unstrained.

• Serve immediately, or store the dressing in a jar, covered, in the refrigerator for up to 3 days.

Avocado Poppy-Seed Dressing

Avocado Ranch Dressing

Avocado Green Goddess Dressing

AVOCADO RANCH DRESSING

I like recipes that don't use up half of my kitchen equipment. This avocadolicious take on ranch dressing just takes a spoon, a knife, and a jar. Dump everything in and shake. Dressing done.

MAKES ABOUT 1 CUP DRESSING

1 mashed avocado
½ cup buttermilk
1 clove garlic, minced
1 teaspoon finely
  chopped chives
1 teaspoon chopped
  fresh dill
1 teaspoon Dijon
  mustard

1 teaspoon lemon
  zest
1 teaspoon apple
  cider vinegar
Sea salt and freshly
  ground black
  pepper

• In a 1-pint mason jar, put the avocado. Add the buttermilk, garlic, chives, dill, mustard, lemon zest, and vinegar. Shake the jar until the dressing looks smooth, creamy, and green. Open the jar, and season the dressing with the salt and pepper to taste.

• Serve immediately, or store the jar, covered, in the refrigerator for up to 3 days.

AVOCADO POPPY-SEED DRESSING

This poppy-seed dressing breathes life into just about any salad or slaw. Try it mixed into a slaw of shredded cabbage, kale, apple, and raw sweet potato matchsticks. Yum!

MAKES ABOUT 1 CUP DRESSING

¼ cup white wine or cider vinegar

2 tablespoons sugar

1 small shallot

2 tablespoons avocado

1 tablespoon poppy seeds

½ teaspoon kosher salt

½ teaspoon ground mustard

¼ cup avocado oil or extra-virgin olive oil

• In the bowl of a food processor, put the vinegar and sugar. Using a microplane or the smallest holes on a box grater, grate the shallot into the bowl. Add the poppy seeds, salt, avocado, and mustard. Pulse, scraping down the sides as needed, until well combined. With the food processor on, stream in the oil and pulse until combined.

• Store the dressing in an airtight container in the refrigerator for up to 1 week.

AVOCADO COMPOUND BUTTER

Spread this butter on your toast, dollop it on a baked sweet potato, or smear it on a juicy grilled steak (see page 143). This easy-to-make compound butter keeps exceptionally well and is a great use for any little leftover bits of avocado.

MAKES ½ CUP BUTTER

¼ cup (½ stick)
   unsalted butter,
   softened

¼ cup avocado,
   fresh or frozen and
   defrosted (see
   page 13)

½ teaspoon lime zest

½ teaspoon kosher
   salt

Pinch of ground avo-
   cado leaf (optional)

• In the bowl of a food processor, pulse all of the ingredients until smooth, scraping down the sides of the bowl as needed.

• Store the butter in an airtight container in the refrigerator for up to 2 weeks.

AVOCADO LEAF SALT

Avocado leaf imparts a subtle anise flavor to this salt, which makes it a nice upgrade to traditional salt-rimmed cocktails and a great finishing salt on any grilled meats or veggies.

MAKES ¼ CUP SALT

¼ cup coarse salt
3 to 4 avocado
   leaves, stemmed

- In a spice grinder, grind the salt with the avocado leaves. Grind as finely as possible, and then use a fine-mesh strainer to filter out any remaining large bits of avocado leaf. Store the salt in an airtight container for up to several months.

appetizers & sides

VEGAN CARPACCIO

Carpaccio was first on a menu at Harry's Bar in Venice, Italy, and named after the painter Vittore Carpaccio, whose Renaissance paintings featured the same rich red color of his foodie namesake. That dish was a simple serving of thinly sliced, raw beef with a dressing of lemon, olive oil, and Parmesan. This carpaccio has many more ingredients than the original but still shares those same rich Renaissance colors.

MAKES 4 SERVINGS

8 thin slices red onion

1 medium red bell pepper

1 avocado, cut into 8 slices

½ small serrano pepper or jalapeño, thinly cut into rounds

1 (4-inch) piece English cucumber, peeled

1 (3-inch) piece heart of palm

About 6 cherry tomatoes, halved

¼ cup sweet corn

About 1 tablespoon avocado oil or extra-virgin olive oil

About 1 tablespoon freshly squeezed lime juice

10 to 15 fresh cilantro leaves, lightly chopped

Microgreens, for garnish

Flakey sea salt and freshly ground black pepper

• Preheat the broiler to high.

• In a small bowl of cold water, place the onion slices. Set aside.

• Cut the bell pepper in half, remove the seeds and pith, and place the halves cut side down on a baking sheet. Broil the bell pepper on high until the skins have blistered and are somewhat blackened, 8 to 10 minutes, checking frequently. Remove the baking sheet from the oven, and allow the bell pepper to cool before removing the blackened skins. Slice each peeled pepper into four pieces, and place them on a serving plate (or two pieces each on four plates).

• Place the avocado slices on top of the pepper slices. Using a vegetable peeler, peel the cucumber and heart of palm into long, thin strips. Spread the strips around the serving plate or divide them among four individual plates, and then top them with the tomatoes and corn. Drain the red onion, and spread it on top.

• Drizzle the vegetables with the oil, and squeeze the lime juice over the top. Sprinkle them with the cilantro, microgreens, salt, and pepper, and serve immediately.

CEVICHE NIKKEI

Nikkei cuisine is the fusion of Japanese dishes with the techniques and ingredients of Peru. This simple ceviche recipe continues that tradition with a touch of ponzu, nori, and avocado.

MAKES 2 TO 3 SERVINGS

For the marinade:

¼ cup freshly squeezed lime juice (from about 2 medium to large limes)

1 clove garlic

1 (1-inch) piece fresh ginger, peeled

½ medium serrano pepper, seeded and finely chopped

2 teaspoon ponzu

1 teaspoon mirin

———————

½ small sweet potato (about ½ pound)

2 thin slices red onion

¼ to ½ pound previously frozen sea bass or other semi-firm white ocean fish, cut into bite-size pieces

Pinch of sea salt

½ avocado, cut into bite-size cubes

1 sheet nori, cut into ¼-inch strips

• To make the marinade, in a small bowl, put the lime juice, garlic, ginger, pepper, ponzu, and mirin. Cover and refrigerate until needed or up to overnight.

• In a medium pot over high heat, bring about 3 cups of water to a boil with a pinch of salt. Boil the sweet potato until you can easily pierce it with a fork, 20 to 30 minutes. Remove the sweet potato from the water, and allow it to cool to room temperature, about 15 minutes. Cut the cooled potato in half lengthwise and then into bite-size pieces.

• In small bowl filled with ice water, soak the onion slices for 10 minutes.

• In a medium bowl, place the sea bass and sprinkle it with the salt. Stir to coat, and let it sit for 2 minutes. Remove the garlic and ginger from the marinade, and pour the mixture over the fish. Let it sit until the fish is opaque, 2 minutes more.

• Drain the water from the onion, and dry on a paper towel. In a new medium bowl, add the onion, avocado, sweet potato, and sea bass, and mix gently. Garnish it with the nori, and serve immediately.

FRESH SALAD ROLLS

Once you get the knack for rolling up these fresh salad rolls, you'll want to skip those prepackaged versions that tend to dry out. I love freshly cooked (but cooled) shrimp in my salad rolls, but there's plenty to fill up these rolls without them.

MAKES 5 ROLLS

2 tablespoons freshly squeezed lime juice (from about 1 lime)

2 tablespoons rice wine vinegar

1 teaspoon sugar

1 teaspoon fish sauce

¼ teaspoon sea salt

1 medium carrot, peeled and cut into 5 matchsticks

3 ounces rice vermicelli noodles

5 (8½-inch) rice paper sheets

5 medium butter lettuce leaves

1 small cucumber, peeled and cut into 5 wedges

5 stems fresh cilantro

¾ cup bean sprouts

½ avocado, cut into 5 wedges

10 cooked shrimp, peeled and deveined (optional)

¼ cup chopped roasted peanuts (optional)

For the peanut dipping sauce:

¼ cup crunchy or creamy peanut butter

¼ cup water

2 tablespoons soy sauce

1 tablespoon brown sugar

Sriracha

• In a medium bowl, mix together the lime juice, vinegar, sugar, fish sauce, and salt.

• In a medium pot over high heat, bring about 3 cups of water to a boil. Blanch the carrots for 1 minute, remove them from the water, and place them in the lime juice mixture. Set aside.

• In a medium bowl, put the noodles and pour the water you used for the carrots over the noodles. Let it sit for 2 minutes, and then drain. Set the noodles aside.

• To assemble the rolls, fill a large bowl with warm water. To make each roll, dip one rice paper sheet into the water. Use a towel to slightly dry the sheet, and then lay the sheet flat on your working surface. Place one of the lettuce leaves just off center, and top it with one-fifth of the noodles, a carrot, a cucumber wedge, a stem of cilantro, a small handful of bean sprouts, and an avocado wedge. Top it with the shrimp and sprinkle it with some peanuts.

• Fold the bottom of the rice paper up over the filling, and then fold in from the sides. Begin rolling it up tightly from the bottom to the top. Press the edges to seal. Set the roll on a plate and cover it with a damp towel while you repeat with the remaining rice paper sheets. If you aren't eating the rolls immediately, wrap them individually in plastic wrap, and refrigerate for up to 1 day.

• Serve these rolls with a peanut dipping sauce.

• To make the dipping sauce, mix together the peanut butter, water, soy sauce, and brown sugar. Add sriracha to taste for a bit of a kick.

SPINACH AVOCADO PHYLLO ROLLS

Because the avocado is hidden away within layers of phyllo, it's protected from the heat and won't get bitter like some cooked avocados . . . it just gets slightly warm and unbelievably creamy. Try them with a little bit of Avocado Chutney (page 63).

MAKES 4 SERVINGS

½ avocado, cut into quarters lengthwise

2 ounces firm feta

2 tablespoons avocado oil or melted unsalted butter, plus more for brushing the dough

4 (8-by-10-inch) sheets of phyllo dough

1 cup packed baby spinach

• Preheat the oven to 350 degrees F and line a baking sheet with parchment paper.

• Cut the feta into four pieces, approximately ½ inch wide and 3 inches long.

• Lay a piece of the phyllo dough on a flat working surface, short side facing you. Fold it in half to create a 4-by-10-inch rectangle.

Brush with the avocado oil. (Make sure to keep the other phyllo pieces covered before using.)

• Place a quarter of the spinach, one piece of avocado, and one piece of feta toward the bottom of the phyllo, and roll the phyllo over the filling, continuing to roll it until you reach the end. Gently pinch the ends to seal, and place the rolls on the prepared baking sheet. Repeat with the remaining ingredients.

• Brush the top of each roll with a bit more oil, and then bake the rolls until golden, about 15 to 20 minutes. Let the rolls cool for 5 minutes and serve warm.

AVO DEVILED EGGS

Deviled eggs may be a 1950s classic, but they can be traced way back to Ancient Rome, where peppery egg yolks were stuffed back into their cooked white. This mayo-free, avocado-stuffed egg takes a note from those spicy stuffed eggs of old by adding a little jalapeño. Of course, you can also use avocado in your favorite traditional deviled egg recipe; simply replace the mayo with avocado. Both are delicious!

MAKES 1 DOZEN DEVILED EGG HALVES

6 large eggs
½ cup smashed
  avocado, fresh
  or frozen and
  defrosted (see
  page 13)
2 tablespoons avo-
  cado oil or olive oil
2 teaspoons apple
  cider vinegar

¼ teaspoon Dijon or
  yellow mustard
1 tablespoon seeded
  and chopped
  jalapeño
1 tablespoon chopped
  fresh cilantro
Sea salt
Smoked paprika,
  for garnish

• In the bottom of a medium pot, place the eggs and cover them with 2 inches of cold water. Bring the pot to a boil. Remove the pan from the heat, and let the eggs sit in the water for 10 minutes. Remove the eggs from the water, let the them cool, and then peel them. Slice each egg in half lengthwise, remove the yolks, and place the yolks into the bowl of a food processor. Set the whites cut side up on a serving plate.

• Add the avocado, oil, vinegar, and mustard to food processor with the egg yolks, and pulse until smooth. Add in the jalapeño and cilantro and pulse twice. Season with salt to taste.

• Scoop 1 tablespoon of the yolk mixture into each egg white half. Dust them with the paprika and serve immediately, or store the eggs, covered, in the refrigerator up to overnight.

MUSHY AVO PEAS

I grew up eating peas from a can. They were more gray than green and tasted like nothing. I was not happy when they showed up on my plate. I would have been a lot more excited about these sweet and creamy mushy avo peas (even with my youthful aversion to avocado). Try serving them along side the Fish and Avo Chips (page 138)!

MAKES 4 SERVINGS

1 tablespoon avocado oil or unsalted butter

1 tablespoon chopped yellow onion

2 cups sweet peas

5 fresh mint leaves, finely chopped

2 tablespoons water

1 avocado, fresh or frozen and defrosted (see page 13)

1 tablespoon freshly squeezed lemon juice

Sea salt

• In a heavy-bottomed pot over low heat, heat the oil and onion until the onion softens, about 10 minutes. Add the peas, mint, and water, and stir. Increase the heat to medium, and cook for 10 minutes more. Remove the pot from the heat.

• In the bowl of a food processor, add the avocado, lemon juice, and half of the cooked peas, and process until the mixture is smooth. Add the remaining peas, and pulse to just combine.

• Add salt to taste, and return the pea mixture to the pot. Rewarm the peas over low heat, and then serve immediately.

• Store any leftovers in an airtight container in the refrigerator for up to 3 days.

BITE-SIZE AVOCADO & SALMON TARTS

Making puff pastry shells from frozen puff pastry is a lot more work than it's worth, so I recommend just starting with the frozen shells in the first place. Then, it's just a quick bake and stuff for these bite-size tart spins on a California roll.

MAKES 1 DOZEN TARTS

12 puff pastry shells

About 2 tablespoons Kewpie Avocado Mayo (see tip on page 59)

12 (1-inch) squares smoked salmon lox

½ avocado, thinly sliced

1 small cucumber, peeled and diced

1 teaspoon chopped chives

• Bake the shells until golden according to the manufacturer's instructions. Cool the shells completely on a wire rack.

• Once they have cooled, top each shell with a smear of the mayo, a piece of the smoked salmon, a few avocado slices, cucumber, and chives. Serve immediately.

GRILLED OYSTERS

Although I usually prefer to slurp my oysters raw, I'm addicted to these lightly grilled, slightly spicy treats. Great meaty oysters, like the Pacific oyster, are essential.

MAKES 1 DOZEN OYSTERS

¼ cup finely grated Parmesan cheese

1 tablespoon finely chopped fresh parsley

1 teaspoon Worcestershire sauce

½ teaspoon hot sauce

12 fresh oysters on the half shell

½ avocado, finely diced

1 teaspoon chopped chives

1 teaspoon freshly squeezed lemon juice

• Preheat the grill to 450 degrees F.

• In a small bowl, place the Parmesan, parsley, Worcestershire, and hot sauce and stir to combine.

• Top each of the opened oysters with a spoonful of the Parmesan mixture. Grill the oysters, uncovered, until the edges of the oysters begin to curl, about 7 minutes.

• In a small bowl, stir together the avocado, chives, and lemon juice until combined. Remove the oysters from the grill and top with the avocado mixture. Serve immediately.

PAN CON AGUACATE

You may be familiar with *pan con tomate,* the toasty bread smeared with crushed tomatoes that just start to seep into the bread. It's completely addictive. And so is this version, with avocado taking the place of the tomato. These toasts are velvety, with a nice brightness from the *boquerónes.*

MAKES 6 SLICES

1 (6-inch) piece baguette, cut on an angle into 6 slices

1 avocado

2 tablespoons avocado oil or extra-virgin olive oil, divided

1 clove garlic

2 *boquerónes,* finely chopped (optional)

Smoked sea salt

- Preheat the oven to 500 degrees F.

- Place the baguette slices on a baking sheet and toast until golden brown, about 5 minutes.

- While the bread is toasting, grate the avocado with a cheese grater into a small bowl. Gently mix the avocado with 1 tablespoon of the oil.

- Remove the baking sheet from the oven, then rub the toasts with the clove of garlic and drizzle them with the remaining 1 tablespoon oil. Divide the *boquerónes* between the toasts, spread the grated avocado on top, then sprinkle them with the salt to taste. Serve immediately.

CALIFORNIA ONION AVO

It's rumored that French onion dip, or California Dip, was originally developed as a marketing ploy to sell more Lipton Onion Soup Mix. With a nod to that original recipe, the addition of avocado makes this dip even more Californian.

MAKES 4 SERVINGS

1 tablespoon avocado oil or extra-virgin olive oil

1½ cups sliced yellow onion

Kosher salt

1 avocado, halved lengthwise (peel reserved for serving)

½ cup sour cream or unsweetened yogurt

Pita chips, for serving

• In a medium skillet over medium-low heat, heat the oil and then add the onion and salt. Slowly cook the onion until it caramelizes, about 20 minutes. Remove the pan from the heat and let the onion cool to room temperature.

• In the bowl of a food processor, place the avocado, sour cream, and caramelized onions, and puree until mostly smooth. Season with salt to taste.

• Return the mixture to the avocado peel, and serve with pita chips, or cover well and refrigerate up to overnight.

LABNEH STUFFED AVOCADO

This combination of avocado, *labneh,* and *dukkah* also makes a great Mediterranean-inspired dip served with pita chips. Just mash the *labneh* and oil into the avocado and then sprinkle with the *dukkah* to serve.

MAKES 1 SERVING

1 avocado

2 tablespoons Labneh (recipe follows)

About 2 teaspoons avocado oil or extra-virgin olive oil

1 teaspoon Dukkah (recipe follows)

• Slice your avocado in half lengthwise, and gently remove the pit. Slice the flesh of the avocado into cubes, leaving it in the peel. Place about 1 tablespoon of the *labneh* in the center of each avocado half, and then drizzle them with the oil. Sprinkle the *labneh* with the *dukkah,* and serve immediately.

CONTINUED

labneh

Labneh is an easy-to-make and incredibly delicious fresh, home-made yogurt cheese. Although you need to start the cheese the day before, there's hardly any active prep time involved. This recipe makes extra yogurt cheese that is delicious spread on toast or used as a dip for fresh veggies or chips. Leave out the garlic if you want to use any extra *labneh* as a spread with a fruity jam.

MAKES ABOUT 1 CUP *LABNEH*

1 cup unsweetened, full-fat Greek yogurt

¼ cup avocado oil or extra-virgin olive oil

¼ teaspoon kosher salt

Pinch of freshly ground black pepper

1 clove garlic, minced (optional)

• In a medium bowl, mix together the yogurt, oil, salt, and pepper, and add the garlic. Double line a fine-mesh strainer with cheesecloth, leaving extra cheesecloth overhanging the sides of the strainer, and place the strainer over a medium bowl. Pour the yogurt mixture on top of the cheesecloth. Pick up the cheesecloth edges, and bundle them together to cover the top of the yogurt. Set aside at room temperature for at least 24, and up to 48, hours, checking occasionally to ensure that the bottom of the strainer is not hanging in any strained liquid (dump out the bowl if it is).

• Remove the *labneh* from the cheese-cloth, place it in an airtight container, and refrigerate for up to a week.

dukkah

This traditional Egyptian spice-and-nut mixture adds both texture and a pop of flavor to whatever you sprinkle it on. Use the extra on top of slices of crusty bread dunked into extra-virgin olive oil, or you can store it in an airtight container in the refrigerator for several weeks. Slices of avocado dipped directly in the *dukkah* mixture are also fantastic.

MAKES ABOUT ⅓ CUP *DUKKAH*

¼ cup roasted hazelnuts, skins removed

2 tablespoons sesame seeds

1 tablespoon coriander seeds

1 tablespoon cumin seeds

1 teaspoon kosher salt

½ teaspoon whole peppercorns

- In the bowl of a food processor or spice grinder, put the hazelnuts, and pulse once or twice until coarsely broken. Add the sesame seeds, coriander seeds, cumin seeds, salt, and peppercorns, and pulse to make a coarse powder. Store in an airtight container at room temperature for up to a month.

salads, soups & sandwiches

CARROT, APPLE & AVOCADO SALAD

When Chef Joshua McFadden (Portland's Ava Gene's) adds a new salad to his menu, it's not to be missed. His giardini marry fresh veggies, fruits, nuts, and acid in ways you'll wonder how you ever lived without. This salad is inspired by one of my favorites, pairing carrot, apple, and avocado with pistachios two ways.

MAKES 2 SIDE SERVINGS

2 medium carrots, cut into ribbons lengthwise with a vegetable peeler

½ medium apple, sliced into wedges

1 tablespoon freshly squeezed lemon juice

1 tablespoon avocado oil or extra-virgin olive oil

1 tablespoon Pistachio Butter (recipe follows)

¼ large avocado, sliced into wedges

2 tablespoons chopped roasted, salted pistachios

Lightly chopped carrot greens, for garnish

Flakey sea salt, for garnish

• In a medium bowl, toss the carrot and apple with the lemon juice, and then drizzle with the oil. Stir in the pistachio butter, and mix to coat.

• Place the carrot and apple mixture on a plate, interspersing the avocado wedges. Sprinkle with the pistachios, and garnish with the carrot greens and salt. Serve immediately.

CONTINUED

pistachio butter

If you don't feel like making your own pistachio butter and you can't find it at the store, cashews and cashew butter make a good substitution.

MAKES ABOUT 1 CUP PISTACHIO BUTTER

1 cup roasted, salted pistachios, shelled
½ cup boiling water
1 tablespoon coconut oil
¼ teaspoon kosher salt

• In a medium bowl, put the pistachios and pour the boiling water over the top. Let them sit for 15 minutes to soften.

• Pour the pistachios and soaking liquid into a food processor or blender along with the oil and salt. Blend until smooth, stopping periodically to scrape down the sides of the bowl. It may take about 15 minutes to fully blend.

• Use immediately or store in an airtight container in the refrigerator for up to 1 week.

AVOCADO & ARTICHOKES

It really doesn't take much to make a great side when you start with great avocados. Some artichoke hearts and green goddess dressing, for example, is all you need.

MAKES 4 SIDE SERVINGS

1 avocado, cut in half
  lengthwise
1 (13-ounce) can quar-
  tered marinated
  artichoke hearts,
  drained

⅛ cup Avocado
  Green Goddess
  Dressing (page 66)
Flakey sea salt and
  freshly ground
  black pepper

• Cut each avocado half into eighths, and put them in a medium bowl. Add the artichoke hearts, and then spoon in the dressing. Lightly stir to coat, and serve immediately, with the salt and pepper to taste.

GOLDEN BEET, WHITE ANCHOVY, AVOCADO & CRISPY FARRO SALAD

There's a lot going on in this hearty salad inspired by one of my favorite Seattle restaurants Staple & Fancy. It has a hit of brightness from the beets and vinegar, a little smoke from the paprika, and a punch of the ocean from the anchovy.

Be sure to use white anchovies, which will be found near the deli in your shop, instead of the canned variety. If you can't find them, leave them out, or substitute in one finely chopped canned anchovy, since the flavor is much stronger.

MAKES 4 SERVINGS

1 pound golden beets

½ cup farro

1 teaspoon sea salt, divided, plus more for serving

2 tablespoons cooking oil (avocado or peanut oil)

½ teaspoon smoked paprika

Pinch of freshly ground black pepper

2 tablespoons salad oil (avocado or extra-virgin olive oil), divided

1 tablespoon red wine vinegar

1 to 2 avocados, halved

8 to 10 white anchovy fillets

¼ cup fresh flat-leaf parsley, for garnish

¼ cup fresh mint, for garnish

About 1 tablespoon freshly squeezed lemon juice

• Scrub the beets well, and place them in a large pot with 4 cups of cold water. Bring the pot to a boil over high heat, cover, reduce the heat to medium low, and simmer until the beets are soft, 30 to 60 minutes. Drain the beets and rinse them in cool water. Set aside to cool to room temperature.

• In a medium pot over high heat, bring 2 cups of water to a boil. Add the farro and ½ teaspoon of the salt. Reduce the heat to medium high and cook the farro until it is very tender, 25 to 30 minutes. Strain the farro and place it on a linen or paper towel (don't use terry cloth, as the farro will get lost in the weave) to dry as much as possible.

CONTINUED

• In a small pot over medium heat, heat the cooking oil. Add the dried farro, and cook, shaking the pan, until the farro starts to smell a bit nutty and pops, about 5 minutes. Cover and cook 2 minutes more, shaking the pot occasionally as though you were making popcorn. Remove the pot from the heat, and add the paprika, the remaining ½ teaspoon salt, and the pepper and toss to coat the farro.

• When the beets are cool, peel off any tough skin, and cut them into halves or quarters (whatever size makes a nice bite), and then put them in a medium bowl. Add 1 tablespoon of the salad oil, the vinegar, and salt and pepper to taste. Toss to coat.

• Slice each avocado half into fourths. Peel and then cut the avocado into smaller bites if needed. Scatter the avocado, beets, and anchovy fillets around four plates. Spread the farro evenly across the top, and garnish with the parsley and mint. Drizzle on the remaining 1 tablespoon salad oil and the lemon juice. Sprinkle with the salt and pepper to taste and serve immediately.

NOTE: If you can't find farro (wheat berries) in your grocery store, try this recipe with pearled barley.

MANGO & CHILI SALAD

Mango and avocado play off each other beautifully, especially with a spike of lime juice and chili flakes. It's a combination you could easily get addicted to.

MAKES 2 SERVINGS

1 medium mango, peeled and cut into ½-inch dice

1 avocado, cut into ½-inch dice

2 tablespoons freshly squeezed lime juice

2 teaspoons lime zest

Pinch of chili flakes

Pinch of flakey sea salt

2 tablespoons chopped fresh mint leaves

2 tablespoons chopped fresh cilantro leaves

• In a medium bowl, add the mango, avocado, and lime juice and zest. Stir to coat. Just before serving, sprinkle with the chili flakes and salt, and garnish with the mint and cilantro.

AHI POKE

Wakame is a dried seaweed that is readily available in most Asian food aisles in the supermarket. If you can't find it, feel free to make this recipe without it.

Be sure to use the highest quality sashimi-grade tuna for your poke, which was flash-frozen at the source (unless, of course, you live at the source!).

MAKES 4 APPETIZER SERVINGS

1 teaspoon wakame (optional)

1 sashimi-grade Ahi tuna steak (about ½ pound), cut into ½-inch cubes

½ avocado, diced

1 tablespoon soy sauce

1½ teaspoons chopped green onion, light-green part included

1 teaspoon sliced shallot

½ teaspoon toasted sesame oil

Splash of chili oil

½ teaspoon sesame seeds, for garnish

• In a small bowl, cover the wakame with warm water and soak for 5 to 10 minutes. Drain and set aside.

• In a medium nonreactive bowl, place the wakame, tuna, avocado, soy sauce, green onion, shallot, sesame oil, and chili oil. Lightly toss to coat.

• Garnish with the sesame seeds and serve immediately, or you can store the salad in an airtight container in the refrigerator up to overnight.

AVOCADO CHICKEN SALAD

If you rarely roast a whole chicken because you don't know what you'd do with the leftovers, this chicken salad recipe may just give you the needed motivation. It's also great with leftover turkey!

MAKES 2 SERVINGS

1 cup shredded
  cooked chicken
¼ cup chopped
  grapes
3 tablespoons
  Avocado Mayo
  (page 59)
1 tablespoon chopped
  fresh tarragon

1 tablespoon toasted,
  salted pepitas
  or nuts
1 teaspoon freshly
  squeezed lemon
  juice
1 green onion,
  thinly sliced
Sea salt and freshly
  ground black
  pepper

• In a medium bowl, put the chicken, grapes, mayo, tarragon, pepitas, lemon juice, and green onion, and stir gently to coat. Add the salt and pepper to taste.

• Serve immediately, or cover and refrigerate up to overnight.

AVOCADO TUNA SALAD

I'm rather picky about tuna salad. To me it shouldn't be sweet or smothered in mayo. This tuna salad is light, with just enough avocado mayo to hold the mixture together. It's just as good in a sandwich as it is on it's own.

MAKES 1 SERVING

3 to 4 tablespoons
   Avocado Mayo
   (page 59)
1 teaspoon apple
   cider vinegar
½ teaspoon Dijon or
   yellow mustard

1 (4-ounce) can tuna,
   drained
1 tablespoon chopped
   yellow onion
1 tablespoon chopped
   dill pickle
Sea salt

• In a medium bowl, put the avocado mayo, mustard, and vinegar, and mix with a fork until smooth. Add the tuna, onion, and pickle, and stir gently to coat. Add salt to taste.

• Serve immediately, or cover and refrigerate up to overnight.

TEQUILA, CITRUS & GINGER STUFFED AVOCADO

Tequila comes in all varieties, some of which are pretty much only good for causing a hangover, while others are deliciously sippable. You'll want the latter for this recipe! If you can find it, I highly recommend Don Julio 70, which is good enough to nip on while you are cooking, no salt or lime needed.

MAKES 2 SERVINGS

½ ounce silver tequila
½ teaspoon grated
  ginger
1 medium orange
1 medium grapefruit
2 teaspoons avocado
  oil or extra-virgin
  olive oil

1 avocado
A few fresh mint
  leaves, for garnish
Flakey sea salt,
  for garnish

• In a medium bowl, put the tequila and ginger. Let it sit for at least 5 minutes.

• Next, supreme the citrus. To do this, cut the top and bottom off the orange and grapefruit, and set them each with one of the cut sides down. Use a chef's knife to cut off the peel, slicing from top to bottom, taking off the pith as well as the peel. Once peeled, use the knife to cut out the sections, leaving behind the membrane between sections. Place the sections in the bowl with the tequila. Stir in the oil.

• Slice the avocado in half lengthwise, and remove the pit. Slice each avocado half, still in the peel, lengthwise four times, and then across four times, without puncturing the peel. Use a spoon to loosen the cut avocado, but leave it in the shell.

• Spoon the orange and grapefruit pieces onto the avocado half (you will have some leftover), and sprinkle with the mint and salt to taste. Serve immediately.

CREMA DE AGUACATE

The hot sauce in this recipe doesn't make the soup particularly spicy. It just adds a subtle acid note to cut through some of the cream. I use Louisiana-style Crystal Hot Sauce, but it would be great with Cholula or Tabasco as well.

MAKES 8 SERVINGS

1 tablespoon avocado oil or extra-virgin olive oil
½ cup finely chopped sweet onion
Pinch of sea salt, plus more for seasoning
1 clove garlic, minced
4 cups vegetable or chicken broth
1 avocado leaf (optional)
2 avocados, mashed, fresh or frozen and defrosted (see page 13)

1 tablespoon freshly squeezed lime juice
1 tablespoon chopped fresh cilantro, plus more for garnish
½ cup heavy cream
1 teaspoon hot sauce
Freshly ground black pepper
Roasted, salted pepitas, for garnish (optional)

• In a large pot over medium-low heat, heat the oil. Add the onion and the salt. Slowly cook the onion until caramelized, about 20 minutes, stirring occasionally. Add the garlic, and cook 2 minutes more.

• Stir in the broth and avocado leaf, and simmer for about 5 minutes. Remove the avocado leaf and transfer the soup to a blender along with the avocado, lime juice, and cilantro. Puree until smooth.

• Return the puree to the pot and place it over low heat. Stir in the cream and hot sauce. Season with the salt and pepper to taste. Serve immediately, or for a cold soup, chill for at least 1 hour or up to overnight. Garnish with some pepitas and a bit more chopped cilantro.

SLOW-COOKER CHICKEN STEW

I had visions of simply dumping everything in this recipe into a slow cooker and coming home to a piquant and creamy chicken stew. Not so much. Avocados cooked for long periods of time get terribly bitter. Luckily, it's easy enough to blend fresh avocado right before serving to get the same spicy and luscious stew I dreamed about. This dish is also great topped with shredded cabbage and a bit of chopped green onion.

MAKES 3 SERVINGS

6 boneless chicken thighs

2 quarts water

1 medium yellow onion, sliced

1 medium jalapeño, seeded and sliced

2 cloves garlic

2 tablespoons dried oregano

2 tablespoons chili powder, plus more for serving

2 teaspoons ground cumin

2 teaspoons kosher salt, plus more for seasoning

½ teaspoon freshly ground black pepper, plus more for seasoning

1 avocado, diced, divided

¼ cup shredded cabbage

• In a slow cooker, put the chicken, water, onion, jalapeño, garlic, oregano, chili powder, cumin, salt, and pepper. Cook on low for 6 to 8 hours or on high for 3 to 4 hours.

• Scoop out 2 cups of the broth (avoiding the chicken), and add it to a blender; blend with three-fourths of the avocado until smooth. Stir the blended avocado mixture back into the stew. Season with a bit more salt and pepper to taste.

• Serve immediately, garnished with the remaining avocado, cabbage, and a dusting of chili powder. Refrigerate any leftovers in an airtight container for up to 2 days.

WAFFLED AVOCADO QUESADILLAS

What's better than a cheesy avocado quesadilla made in a waffle iron? You have to try it to believe it. Just be careful to avoid getting cheese in the waffle iron, or you'll have a lot of cleanup to do!

MAKES 1 SERVING

2 flour tortillas, slightly larger than your waffle iron

1 tablespoon avocado oil or melted unsalted butter

¾ cup grated Monterey jack or cheddar cheese

1 avocado, sliced

Pico de gallo (optional)

Sour cream, for serving (optional)

• Heat your waffle iron to medium high per the manufacturer's instructions.

• Place the tortillas down on a flat surface and brush one tortilla with half of the oil.

Place it oil side down on the waffle iron, and layer about half the cheese, the avocado slices, some pico de gallo, and then the remaining cheese. Top with the other tortilla, and quickly brush the remaining oil on the top.

• Cook according to your waffle iron's recommendations, typically 3 minutes.

• Remove the quesadilla from the waffle iron with a fork, and cut it into quarters. Serve immediately, with a bit more pico de gallo and sour cream.

GREEN GAZPACHO

Sometimes eating gazpacho is a bit like eating a bowl of salsa. This green gazpacho is nothing like that. It's slightly sweet, mostly tart, totally refreshing, and belongs nowhere near a corn chip.

MAKES 6 TO 8 SERVINGS

4 cups diced honeydew melon (from about 1 medium melon)

½ cup packed fresh mint, plus more for garnish

2 to 3 tablespoons freshly squeezed lemon juice

2 tablespoons freshly squeezed lime juice

1 medium jalapeño, seeded and chopped

1 clove garlic, minced

2 tablespoons avocado oil or extra-virgin olive oil

1 avocado, diced

1 cup peeled and diced cucumber

¼ cup diced red onion

Sea salt and freshly ground black pepper

- In a blender, puree the melon, mint, citrus juices, jalapeño, and garlic and puree until smooth.

- Transfer the melon mixture to a large bowl, and then stir in the avocado, cucumber, and onion. Season with the salt and pepper to taste. Cover the bowl with plastic wrap, pushing the wrap down to the surface of the soup, and let it sit in the refrigerator for at least 1 hour before serving or up to overnight. Garnish with a bit of fresh mint to serve.

CUBANO SANDWICH

Avocado may not be a part of the classic Cuban sandwich, but I think it should be. Even better, add Avocado Pickles (page 60)!

MAKES 1 SERVING

1 crusty white roll (or Cuban bread, if you can find it)

½ tablespoon yellow mustard

4 to 5 dill pickle slices

1 slice Swiss cheese

½ avocado, thinly sliced

2 slices Cuban Roast Pork Loin (recipe follows)

1 to 2 pieces smoked ham

About 1 tablespoon softened unsalted butter

• Cut the roll in half, and spread the mustard on the cut side of one of the halves. Top with the pickle, cheese, avocado, and roast pork. Fold each slice of ham in half, and place them on top of the roast pork, then finish with the top of the roll.

• Spread the butter evenly across the top and bottom of the bread, and cook in a sandwich press, if you have one, and cook until the bread is golden brown, 4 to 6 minutes. If you don't have a sandwich press, use a skillet with a little more butter, and press down on the sandwich with a spatula while it's cooking. Cook until the bread is golden brown, about 3 minutes on each side.

• Slice the sandwich from corner to corner, and serve immediately.

CONTINUED

cuban roast pork loin

While you can use just about any leftover pork for a delicious Cuban, the sandwich really shines with traditional mojo roast pork. If you make this recipe with a whole pork shoulder instead of the smaller pork loin roast, double the marinade ingredients.

MAKES 1 TO 2 POUNDS PORK LOIN

1 to 2 pounds pork loin roast

½ cup orange juice

¼ cup freshly squeezed lime juice (from about 2 limes)

3 cloves garlic, chopped

1 tablespoon avocado oil or olive oil

1 tablespoon orange zest

1 teaspoon dried oregano

1 teaspoon ground cumin

½ teaspoon sea salt

• In a gallon-size ziplock bag, put all of the ingredients. Seal the bag, rotate it a few times to make sure the marinade is well combined, and then place it in the refrigerator overnight.

• When you are ready to cook, remove the pork from the marinade, and place it in a roasting pan, skin side up. Let it sit at room temperature for about 20 minutes.

• Preheat the oven to 425 degrees F.

• Place the remaining marinade in a small pan over medium-high heat, and bring it to a low boil. Boil the marinade until slightly reduced, about 2 minutes, and then remove the pan from the heat. Set aside.

• Move the pork to the oven, and cook the pork until well browned, about 15 minutes. Reduce the heat to 350 degrees F, and continue to roast the pork, basting occasionally with the reduced marinade, until the internal temperature reaches 150 degrees F, about 40 minutes more. Remove the roasting pan from the oven, and let the pork rest for 15 minutes before slicing. You should have enough pork loin for eight to twelve sandwiches, depending on the size of your roast. Just slice off about a ¼-inch-thick slice when you are ready to make your sandwich, and keep the remaining roast well wrapped and refrigerated until needed, up to 1 week. You can also freeze the roast, well wrapped, for up to 1 month.

mains

Avocado Mac 127

Avocado Green Curry Noodles 129

Quinoa & Edamame Bowl 132

Grilled Avocado Skewers 135

Avocado & Shrimp Fettuccine 136

Fish & Avo Chips 138

Black Cod with Avocado Cauliflower Mash 141

Lamb Chop with Avocado Chutney 142

Grilled Rib Eye with Peppers &
Avocado Compound Butter 145

Thai Stuffed Avocado 146

"Twice Baked" Avocado 148

AVOCADO MAC

Replacing the cheese with avocado makes a just as delicious but far more nutritious twist on golden stovetop mac. Cashew milk, which is easier to make than you may think, makes a fantastic faux-cream sauce if you want to take it all the way to a plant-based dish, but feel free to use regular milk if you prefer.

MAKES 2 SERVINGS

1 cup elbow macaroni or shells

½ cup Cashew Milk (recipe follows) or milk of choice

1 tablespoon coconut oil

2 teaspoons sugar

¼ teaspoon dry mustard

¼ teaspoon onion powder

¼ teaspoon turmeric

⅛ teaspoon paprika

⅓ cup smashed avocado, fresh or frozen and defrosted (see page 13)

1 teaspoon freshly squeezed lemon juice

Kosher salt and freshly ground black pepper

- In a medium pot over high heat, bring about 4 cups of water with a pinch of salt to a boil. Add the pasta and cook according to the package's directions, to al dente.

- While the pasta is cooking, in a small pot over low heat, heat the cashew milk and coconut oil until the coconut oil is just melted. Stir in the sugar, mustard, onion powder, turmeric, and paprika. Remove the pan from the heat, add the avocado and lemon juice, and blend with an immersion blender until smooth. Add the salt and pepper to taste.

- Drain the pasta, and stir it into the avocado cream sauce. Serve immediately.

CONTINUED

cashew milk

Cashew milk makes a great milk substitute in savory sauces. Make sure that you use raw, not roasted and salted, cashews to make your cashew milk.

MAKES ABOUT 1 QUART CASHEW MILK

1 cup raw cashews
Pinch of kosher salt

- In a 1-quart jar, put the cashews, and fill it with water. Cover, and let it sit overnight. Strain the water off of the cashews and discard.

- In a blender, put the softened cashews and add 2 cups of water and the salt. Blend until you can no longer see pieces of cashew, about 3 minutes. Add another cup of water and blend for 1 minute more. For thinner milk, add up to another cup of water. Strain through a fine-mesh strainer or a nut-milk bag, and store the cashew milk in an airtight container in the refrigerator for up to 4 days.

AVOCADO GREEN CURRY NOODLES

Making your own green curry paste is easier than you probably think, but feel free to substitute store-bought if you want. There are some great options available in most grocery stores. If you can't find Thai eggplants, which are small green globes resembling tomatillos, substitute one or two Japanese eggplants cut into four to five pieces.

MAKES 4 SERVINGS

1 tablespoon vegetable oil

4 to 5 Thai eggplants, cut in half

½ cup button mushrooms

½ medium red bell pepper

¼ cup Green Curry Paste (recipe follows)

1 (13-ounce) can coconut milk

1 cup vegetable or chicken broth

1 tablespoon fish sauce

1 teaspoon sugar

4 ounces rice vermicelli noodles

1 avocado, sliced

1 small red Thai chili, thinly sliced on an angle

16 Thai basil leaves

• In a large heavy-based pan over medium heat, heat the oil. Add the eggplant, mushrooms, and pepper and cook until softened, about 5 minutes. Reduce the heat to medium low and add the curry paste. Continue to cook, stirring constantly, until fragrant, about 3 minutes.

• Add the thick cream from the can of coconut (reserving the rest), and cook for 10 minutes more. Add the broth, fish sauce, sugar, and the rest of the liquid from the coconut milk can, and simmer for 10 minutes more.

• In a medium bowl, put the vermicelli noodles, and pour 2 to 3 cups of boiling water over the noodles. Let the noodles sit for 2 minutes, and then drain.

• When cool enough to handle, twist the noodles into small nests, and divide them between four bowls. Top the noodles with plenty of the green curry mixture, avocado slices, chili slices, and Thai basil leaves.

CONTINUED

green curry paste

This green curry paste can be pretty hot, depending on your Thai chilies. If you like your curries milder, decrease the number of chilies.

MAKES ABOUT ½ CUP CURRY PASTE

10 green Thai chilies
2 medium shallots
2 cloves garlic
1 (4-inch) piece lemongrass, sliced into rounds
1 (1-inch) piece galangal or ginger

1 tablespoon fish sauce
1 tablespoon vegetable oil, plus more as needed
1 teaspoon lime zest

• Using a mortar and pestle or small food processor, blend all of the ingredients to make a smooth paste. If needed, add a bit more oil to help blend the mixture.

• Store the curry paste in an airtight container in the refrigerator for up to 2 weeks.

QUINOA & EDAMAME BOWL

This sweet-and-savory bowl is bursting with Mediterranean spices. If you can't find preserved lemons, feel free to substitute fresh lemon zest along with a hearty pinch of salt.

MAKES 2 SERVINGS (OR 6 SIDE SERVINGS)

½ cup quinoa

2 heaping table-
   spoons dried
   currants

1 tablespoon finely
   chopped preserved
   lemon peel

1 clove garlic

2 tablespoons avo-
   cado oil or extra-
   virgin olive oil

2 tablespoons freshly
   squeezed lemon
   juice

½ teaspoon ground
   coriander

¼ teaspoon ground
   cinnamon

Pinch of ground
   cloves

1 cup edamame

½ fennel bulb,
   thinly sliced

1 avocado, diced

¼ cup chopped pista-
   chios, for garnish

• In a medium pot over medium-high heat, add the quinoa and cover it with about 3 cups of water. Bring the pot to the boil, stir once, and then reduce the heat to medium and simmer for 15 minutes more, until the quinoa is cooked but al dente. Drain well, and set it aside to dry and cool.

• While the quinoa is cooking, in a small bowl, put the currants and cover them with hot water. Let the currants sit for 5 minutes, and then drain. Set aside.

• In a medium bowl, whisk together the lemon peel, garlic, oil, lemon juice, coriander, cinnamon, and cloves. When the quinoa has cooled, add it to the lemon dressing, and stir to coat. Toss in the currants, edamame, fennel, and avocado and gently mix. Garnish with pistachios and serve immediately, or cover and refrigerate up to 2 days.

GRILLED AVOCADO SKEWERS

Avocados don't have to sit on the sidelines! A couple of these veggie skewers are hearty enough to be a main course. Be sure that your avocados are ripe but on the firm side, or you'll end up with too much of a mush.

MAKES 2 SERVINGS

1 large, firm avocado
1 medium bell pepper, cut into half, then eighths
1 small red onion, cut into 2-inch wedges
8 button mushrooms
2 tablespoons freshly squeezed lemon juice

1 tablespoon avocado oil or extra-virgin olive oil
Pinch of flakey sea salt
Pinch of smoked paprika

• Soak four 12-inch wooden skewers in water for at least 15 minutes.

• Cut each avocado in half, and remove the pit. Slice a little of the top of the avocado off, and gently pull off the peel, leaving the half intact. Then, cut each half into eights, with one slice top to bottom and then three slices across.

• Preheat your grill to medium heat.

• Thread the avocado, bell pepper, onion, and mushrooms onto the skewers, only one type per skewer (the veggies need to cook for different times, so it's best not to alternate).

• Place the skewers side by side on a plate and sprinkle them with the lemon juice and then brush on the oil.

• Place the mushroom and onion skewers on the grill and grill them for 3 minutes. Rotate, and grill them 3 minutes more.

• Add the bell pepper and avocado skewers to the grill, and cook all four skewers 2 minutes more on each side. Remove the skewers to a serving plate.

• Sprinkle the skewers with the salt and paprika and serve immediately.

AVOCADO & SHRIMP FETTUCCINE

Fettuccine alfredo, meet shrimp taco. I think you two will get along beautifully.

MAKES 4 SERVINGS

9 ounces fettuccine

1 avocado

½ medium jalapeño, seeded and chopped

¼ cup water

1 tablespoon avocado oil or canola oil, divided

1 tablespoon chopped fresh oregano or marjoram

1 tablespoon freshly squeezed lime juice

1 teaspoon lime zest

½ teaspoon sea salt, plus more for seasoning

½ pound shrimp, peeled and deveined

Freshly ground black pepper

1 tablespoon minced garlic

½ cup queso fresco, for serving

Lime wedges, for serving

Cilantro, for serving

• In a large pot over high heat, bring about 6 cups of water with a pinch of salt to a boil. Add the pasta and cook according to the package's directions, to al dente. Drain the pasta and set it aside.

• While the pasta is cooking, in the bowl of a food processor, pulse the avocado three times. Add the jalapeño, water, 1 teaspoon of the oil, the oregano, lime juice and zest, and salt and pulse until smooth. Set aside.

• Season the shrimp with the salt and pepper to taste.

• In a large skillet over medium heat, heat the remaining 2 teaspoons oil. Add the shrimp and cook for 2 minutes on each side. Stir in the garlic, reduce the heat to low, and simmer for 5 minutes, until the garlic is fragrant and lightly browned all over.

• Toss in the avocado mixture and stir to coat. If the sauce is too thick, add another 1 to 2 tablespoons water and stir to thin. Then, toss in the fettuccine and simmer until just warm.

• Serve immediately with a sprinkle of the queso fresco, the lime wedges, and cilantro.

NOTE: Cutting back on pasta? This dish is also fantastic with zucchini noodles.

FISH & AVO CHIPS

Fried avocado chips are the perfect basket companions to some crispy fish fillets. Just make sure that your oil stays at the right temperature, or your fried goodies could get greasy.

MAKES 1 SERVING

Safflower oil, for
  deep-frying
2 to 3 white fish
  fillets (about
  ½ pound total)
About ½ teaspoon
  sea salt
About 1 teaspoon
  freshly ground
  black pepper
About 1 cup pale beer,
  without a head
¾ cup unbleached
  all-purpose flour,
  plus more for
  dusting

¼ cup cornstarch
1 teaspoon baking
  powder
2 firm but ripe
  avocados, cut
  into wedges
1 medium lemon, cut
  into wedges and
  seeds removed,
  for serving
Avocado Aioli (see
  tip on page 59),
  for serving

• In a large frying pan (or deep fryer), add about 2 inches of the oil, leaving at least 2 inches from the top of the pan, and heat it to 360 to 370 degrees F.

• Cut the fish fillets into smaller pieces if needed. Season the fillets on both sides with the salt and pepper. Set aside.

• In a large bowl, whisk together the beer, flour, cornstarch, and baking powder until you have a smooth and shiny batter. Dust the fish with a small amount of flour, and then dip it into the batter.

• Carefully place the fish into the hot oil and cook it until golden and crisp, about 2 minutes on each side. You can cook more than one piece of fish at a time, but don't overcrowd the fryer. Repeat with the remaining fish.

• Repeat the process with the avocado wedges, dusting them lightly in flour and then dipping them in the batter and frying them until the batter is golden, about 4 minutes.

• Serve immediately with a wedge of lemon and avocado aioli.

BLACK COD WITH AVOCADO CAULIFLOWER MASH

This recipe looks fancy, but it is stunningly simple. It calls for black cod, just because I think it's delicious, but you can use just about any roasted fresh fish . . . salmon, trout, and halibut are all terrific. You'll have a bit of leftover mash, which keeps great for leftovers the next day.

MAKES 2 SERVINGS

1 small head cauliflower (about 1 pound), coarsely chopped

Sea salt

2 black cod fillets, sizes of your choosing

Freshly ground black pepper

1 teaspoon avocado oil

1 cup smashed avocado, fresh or frozen and defrosted (see page 13)

2 tablespoons unsweetened yogurt

1 teaspoon Avocado Leaf Salt (page 71) or other finishing salt

• In a medium pot over high heat, bring about 4 cups of water to a boil. Add the cauliflower and a pinch of sea salt, and cook until very tender, 15 to 18 minutes. Drain the cauliflower completely, place it in a medium bowl, and set aside.

• Season the cod well with the sea salt and pepper to taste.

• Preheat the oven to 425 degrees F and place a large cast-iron skillet with the oil on the stovetop over medium-high heat.

• When the skillet is hot, add the cod, skin side down, and sear for 2 minutes. Flip the cod, skin side up, and transfer the skillet to the oven. Cook the fillets until the fish is opaque in the center, about 2 minutes more. Be careful not to overcook.

• Add the avocado and yogurt to the cauliflower, and using an immersion blender, puree the mixture until smooth, about 1 minute. Season with the sea salt and pepper to taste, and dollop a healthy serving on the middle of two plates. Top with each serving with a fillet, garnish with the avocado leaf salt, and serve immediately.

LAMB CHOP WITH AVOCADO CHUTNEY

If you can find them, use frenched lamb chops with most of the fat trimmed off for this recipe. The cleaned chop bone makes a great little handle for these meat "lollies" to scoop up plenty of the avocado chutney.

MAKES 4 SERVINGS

¼ cup avocado oil or extra-virgin olive oil

2 tablespoons orange juice

2 tablespoons sherry vinegar

1 clove garlic, crushed

1 teaspoon chopped rosemary

8 lamb chops

Flakey sea salt

¼ cup Avocado Chutney (page 63), for serving

• In a shallow dish, stir together the oil, orange juice, vinegar, garlic, and rosemary. Add the lamb chops and turn to coat. Set aside for 10 minutes to marinate.

• Preheat your grill to high, or use a grill pan on the stovetop over high heat. Cook lamb chops for 3 minutes on each side or until cooked to your liking. Sprinkle with salt to taste, and then let the lamb chops rest for 5 minutes.

• Serve with the avocado chutney.

GRILLED RIB EYE WITH PEPPERS & AVOCADO COMPOUND BUTTER

Use any cut of beef (or even lamb or pork) with this simple rub and a dollop of avocado compound butter for a dinner of champions. But it's really hard to beat a bone-in rib eye for both flavor and tenderness.

MAKES 1 TO 2 SERVINGS

1 bone-in rib eye

¼ teaspoon ground coriander

½ teaspoon ground allspice

¼ teaspoon chili flakes

¼ teaspoon Avocado Leaf Salt (page 71) or sea salt

¼ teaspoon freshly ground black pepper

4 medium serrano or shishito peppers

1 tablespoon Avocado Compound Butter (page 70)

• Let the rib eye stand at room temperature for at least 30 minutes.

• Preheat your grill to medium-high heat, and preheat your oven to 450 degrees F.

• In a small bowl, mix together the coriander, allspice, chili flakes, avocado leaf salt, and pepper and then rub it all over the rib eye.

• When the oven is hot, in a large cast-iron skillet (large enough to hold the steak and peppers), put the peppers, and place the skillet in the oven while the steaks are cooking.

• Grill the steak over medium-high heat for about 2 to 3 minutes, then rotate the steak 45 degrees and cook for 2 minutes more. Repeat on the other side. (If you don't have a grill, you can also cook the rib eye in the cast-iron skillet or grill pan on the stovetop on high heat.)

• Remove the skillet from the oven, and flip the peppers. Transfer the meat to the skillet, return the skillet to the oven, and cook for 5 to 10 minutes, depending on desired doneness. Remove the rib eye and peppers to a cutting board, and let them rest for 10 minutes.

• Serve the rib eye and peppers with the avocado butter on top.

THAI STUFFED AVOCADO

Tamarind paste gives pad thai its signature flavor, and it's hard to replace with anything else. This dish will still be delicious if you have to leave it out, but it won't quite have the same pad thai quality.

MAKES 2 SERVINGS

1 teaspoon freshly squeezed lime juice

1 teaspoon fish sauce

½ teaspoon tamarind paste

½ teaspoon sugar

About 6 peeled, deveined, and cooked shrimp, chopped

1 avocado

2 teaspoons chopped peanuts

2 stems cilantro, chopped, for garnish

1 green onion, sliced into rounds, for garnish

Sriracha, for serving

• In a medium bowl, mix together the fish sauce, lime juice, tamarind paste, and sugar. Add the shrimp and set aside.

• Cut the avocado in half and remove the pit. Carefully remove the peel, keeping the halves intact.

• Top each avocado half with the shrimp mixture, and garnish with the peanuts, cilantro, green onion, and sriracha to taste.

"TWICE BAKED" AVOCADO

If the idea of warm avocado intrigues you, this is a good recipe to start with. Just a little blast under the broiler to melt the cheese warms the dish just enough for the flavors to blend (but not enough to get bitter).

MAKES 2 SERVINGS

2 avocados

2 slices bacon, cooked and chopped

1 green onion, sliced

2 ounces (½ cup) grated cheddar, Monterey jack, or feta cheese, divided

¼ teaspoon flakey sea salt

- Preheat the broiler to high.

- Slice one of the avocados in half lengthwise, and remove the pit. Scoop out the flesh, place it in a medium bowl, and mash it until smooth. Add the bacon, green onion, and ¼ cup of the cheese.

- Slice the remaining avocado in half, and remove the pit. Use a knife to carefully release most of the flesh from the peel, but leave the peel on. Top the avocado halves with the mashed avocado mixture, the remaining ¼ cup cheese, and the salt.

- Place the filled avocados on a baking sheet, and broil until the cheese has melted, about 5 minutes. Serve warm.

desserts

AVOCADO KEY LIME PIE

Can't get key limes? You can make this recipe with regular limes, but it won't be quite as tart. You can also use bottled key lime juice, but don't skimp on the fresh lime zest.

MAKES ONE 9-INCH PIE

For the crust:

1½ cups finely ground graham cracker crumbs (from about 10 squares)

3 tablespoons granulated sugar

2 pinches of sea salt

⅓ cup coconut oil or unsalted butter, melted

———————

2 cups smashed avocado, fresh or frozen and defrosted (see page 13)

½ cup plus 2 tablespoons freshly squeezed key lime juice (from about 5 limes)

½ cup sweetened condensed coconut milk

4 teaspoons key lime zest (from about 2 limes)

1 teaspoon vanilla extract

Pinch of kosher salt

• To make the graham cracker crust, preheat the oven to 350 degrees F.

• In a medium bowl, combine the graham cracker, sugar, and salt. Add the coconut oil and stir until the crumbs are evenly coated. Press the crumbs into the bottom and up the sides of a standard 9-inch pie dish using a spoon or the bottom of a measuring cup. Bake the crust until lightly browned, about 10 minutes. Remove the pie crust from the oven and cool it on a rack in the dish for 15 minutes, and then refrigerate until well chilled, about 1 hour.

• This crust can be tightly wrapped in its dish and frozen for up to 2 weeks. Thaw before using.

• In a blender, blend the avocado, lime juice, condensed milk, lime zest, vanilla, and salt until smooth and silky. Spoon the mixture over the graham cracker crust. Cover and refrigerate the pie for at least 2 hours and preferably overnight.

AVOCADO TRUFFLES

Think you need heavy cream for velvety truffles? Think again. Silky smooth avocado puree does the trick just as well.

MAKES 1 DOZEN TRUFFLES

4 ounces 70 percent dark chocolate, coarsely chopped

3 tablespoons pureed avocado, fresh or frozen and defrosted (see page 13)

Pinch of sea salt

⅛ cup natural unsweetened cocoa powder

> **TIP:** Try adding a couple of drops of mint or other flavored extract (or booze!) to the warm ganache. Truly awesome.

- In a double boiler over a pot of boiling water or in a bowl over warm water, melt the chocolate. Stir in the avocado and salt. As you stir it should thicken to a frosting-like texture.

- Cover and chill the bowl until it thickens, about 25 minutes. Using a melon baller, scoop bite-size pieces of the ganache, and roll them in your hands to form into balls. If the balls just aren't forming, refrigerate the ganache for 30 minutes more.

- In a small bowl, place the cocoa powder, and then roll each of the truffle balls in the cocoa powder to coat. Store them in a cool spot or in an airtight container in the refrigerator.

AVOCADO BRÛLÉE

This is a fun dish to serve in the avocado shell, but only if your avocados are small or you split a single brûlée between two (or more!) people. A little of this rich custard goes a long way.

MAKES 4 SERVINGS

1 cup smashed avocado, fresh or frozen and defrosted (see page 13)

½ cup sweetened condensed coconut milk

½ cup unsweetened almond milk or milk of choice

2 teaspoons vanilla extract

Pinch of kosher salt

About ¼ cup super-fine sugar

- In a blender, puree the avocado, condensed milk, almond milk, vanilla, and salt, until completely smooth and thick.

- Divide the mixture between four 4-ounce ramekins and cover them with plastic wrap. Chill the custard for 30 minutes or up to overnight.

- To serve, sprinkle each ramekin with a tablespoon of the sugar. Move a kitchen blowtorch flame evenly across the sugar until the sugar melts and become slightly browned. Let the brûlée sit for a few minutes to firm before serving.

NOTE: You can skip the brûlée step entirely if you wish; the custard is delicious enough on its own!

CHOCOLATE AVOCADO CAKE

This cake is almost as easy as a box cake, with just a bit more measuring and a lot fewer preservatives, and this chocolate avocado frosting rivals some of the best I've ever tasted. It goes onto your cake like a dream. The recipe makes one very rich, flat cake (or about a dozen cupcakes), so if you want layers, be sure to double it!

MAKES ONE 8- OR 9-INCH CAKE OR 1 DOZEN CUPCAKES

1¼ cups unbleached all-purpose flour

1 cup sugar

⅓ cup natural unsweetened cocoa powder

1 teaspoon baking soda

½ teaspoon kosher salt

1 cup warm water

½ cup avocado, fresh or frozen and defrosted (see page 13)

1 teaspoon vanilla extract

1 teaspoon distilled white or apple cider vinegar

For the Chocolate Avocado Frosting

1½ cups powdered sugar, sifted

1 cup smashed avocado, fresh or frozen and defrosted (see page 13)

3 tablespoons natural unsweetened cocoa powder, sifted

1 teaspoon vanilla extract

½ teaspoon kosher salt

1 to 2 tablespoons coconut oil, melted (optional)

• Preheat the oven to 350 degrees F.

• Line the bottom of an 8-inch square or 9-inch round cake pan with parchment paper, or a twelve-cup cupcake tin with paper liners, and set aside.

• In a medium bowl, whisk together the flour, sugar, cocoa powder, baking soda, and salt. Set aside.

• Using an immersion blender in a medium bowl or a blender, puree the water, avocado, vanilla, and vinegar until smooth. Fold the avocado mixture into the dry mixture until thoroughly combined.

• Pour the batter into the prepared pan, and bake until a knife inserted in the center comes out clean, 25 to 30 minutes.

• Let the cake cool completely before frosting and serving, about 2 hours.

• You can make the cake the day before you need it. Cool the cake completely, and then wrap it in plastic wrap, and store it in the refrigerator. To freeze the cake, place the cooled, unfrosted cake on a baking sheet, unwrapped, in the freezer until firm, about 30 minutes. Then wrap it in plastic wrap so that it's airtight and store it in the freezer for up to several weeks.

• While the cake is cooling, make the frosting. In a blender, blend the powdered sugar, avocado, cocoa powder, vanilla, and salt, scraping down the sides occasionally, until you have a thick and creamy frosting. Since the water content of avocados can vary, if your frosting seems a bit too thin, blend in 1 to 2 tablespoons of melted coconut oil. Transfer the frosting to an airtight container and chill it for at least 20 minutes. As the frosting chills, it will thicken. You can store the frosting in the refrigerator for up to 3 days.

• Spread the frosting on the sides and top of the cake, and serve immediately. Leftover frosted cake can be stored in a cake keeper in the refrigerator for up to 2 days.

AVOCADO & CREAM PALETAS

It may seem strange to have avocado in an ice pop, but avocado pairs surprisingly well with cinnamon and cream. While you can make these with any avocado variety, try fruitier versions like Choquette or Bacon if you can. *Paletas* are typically made in rectangular metallic ice pop molds, but you can use any type of mold in this recipe.

MAKES 4 TO 6 SERVINGS

1 cup whole milk

¼ cup granulated sugar

⅛ teaspoon kosher salt

¾ cup crema (Mexican salted cream) or crème fraîche

3 tablespoons powdered sugar

2 teaspoons freshly squeezed lemon juice, divided

½ teaspoon vanilla extract

¼ cup water

1 tablespoon avocado honey

½ teaspoon ground cinnamon

¾ cup diced avocado

• In a medium pot over medium heat, add the milk, granulated sugar, and salt. Cook, stirring occasionally, until the sugar is dissolved and the mixture comes to a gentle boil. Simmer for 5 minutes more.

• Transfer the milk mixture to a medium bowl. Add the crema, powdered sugar, and 1 teaspoon of the lemon juice, and whisk until smooth. Whisk in the vanilla. Chill the mixture until cold, at least 15 minutes and up to overnight.

• Fill each ice pop mold with 1 inch of the crema mixture. Freeze until the mixture begins to set, about 30 minutes.

• While the crema mixture is freezing, in a small pot over medium-low heat, place the water, honey, cinnamon, and the remaining 1 teaspoon lemon juice, and warm until you have a smooth syrup. Remove the pot from the heat, and gently stir in the avocado to coat. Allow to cool for at least 15 minutes.

• When the ice pops have started to set, divide the avocado among the molds, and then evenly pour the remaining crema mixture into each mold, stopping at least ½ inch from the top of the mold. Use a skewer or chopstick to gently disperse the avocado around the pop.

• Place the lids over the ice pop molds, insert the sticks, and freeze until the ice pops are solid, at least 4 hours.

CHOCOLATE CHIP COOKIES

Avocado is a miracle worker in baked goods, like these chocolate chip cookies. By replacing half of the butter with avocado, you'll get a cookie that stays thick and chewy in the center (but still crisp on the outside).

MAKES ABOUT 2 DOZEN COOKIES

¾ cup packed light brown sugar

½ cup (1 stick) unsalted butter

½ cup smashed avocado, fresh or frozen and defrosted (see page 53)

⅓ cup granulated sugar

⅓ cup turbinado, coconut, or raw sugar

2 large eggs

1 teaspoon vanilla extract

2 cups unbleached all-purpose flour

1 teaspoon baking soda

¾ teaspoon kosher salt

7 to 8 ounces chocolate, chopped

Flaky sea salt, for garnish

• Preheat the oven to 360 degrees F, and line two baking sheets with parchment paper.

• In the bowl of a stand mixer or using a handheld electric mixer, cream the brown sugar, butter, avocado, granulated sugar, and turbinado sugar on medium until light, about 5 minutes. Scrape down the sides of the bowl, and add the eggs one at a time, mixing until well combined between each egg. Mix in the vanilla. Set aside.

• In a medium bowl, whisk together the flour, baking soda, and kosher salt.

• With the mixer on low, use a small measuring cup to add small scoops of the flour mixture to the butter-sugar mixture until just combined. Do not overmix. Fold in the chocolate.

• Scoop out the cookie dough in 1½-tablespoon rounds, and place them on the baking sheets with at least 2 inches between each cookie. Give each round a gentle pat, and sprinkle it with the sea salt.

• Bake until the cookies are golden brown, 12 to 14 minutes. Remove the baking sheets from the oven and let the cookies sit on the baking sheets for a few minutes before transferring the cookies to a cooling rack.

TIP: Don't bake all of these cookies at once, unless you are taking them to a function. You'll die from cookie bliss. Instead, bake just a few. Then scoop the rest onto a baking sheet and freeze them. Once frozen, pop them into an airtight container and store them in the freezer, for ready-to-bake cookies anytime.

drinks

———

BRAZILIAN-STYLE LEMONA-CADO

Brazilian lemonade isn't made from lemons. It's a deliciously tart and creamy mixture of fresh lime and sweetened condensed milk. My take skips the canned milk and uses fresh avocado for an equally creamy but more nutritious sip. (Add a little fresh mint for fun spin on a no-jito.)

MAKES TWO 8-OUNCE SERVINGS

1 large lime
½ avocado, fresh or frozen and defrosted (see page 13)
1½ cups cold water

1 cup ice, plus more for serving
1 to 3 tablespoons agave syrup or honey

TIP: Does your blender get hot trying to crush ice? If so, zest your lime and then juice it instead of putting it whole in the blender, and just stir in some crushed ice.

- Trim the ends off of the lime, and set the ends aside. In a high-powered blender, pulse the lime, avocado, water, ice, and 1 tablespoon of the agave syrup. Pulse until well blended, about 1 minute. You'll still see some flecks of lime peel, but the drink should be a creamy-looking light green.

- Taste and add more agave syrup and pulse a few more times if needed.

- Place a fine-mesh strainer over a pitcher, and pour the drink into the pitcher, using a spoon to gently strain the liquid.

- To serve, pack two glasses with crushed ice, and split the strained drink between them.

- Garnish each glass with a trimmed end from the lime.

AVOCADO-NOG

Super creamy and just lightly sweet, this vegan version of the holiday classic doesn't need to sit in your basement for three months to get you in the holiday spirit. If you have a real sweet tooth, you may want to increase the amount of honey.

MAKES TWO 8-OUNCE SERVINGS

1¾ cups unsweetened almond milk or milk of choice

¼ cup smashed avocado, fresh or frozen and defrosted (see page 13)

2 tablespoons avocado honey or agave syrup

1 teaspoon freshly squeezed lemon juice

½ teaspoon vanilla extract

¼ teaspoon freshly grated nutmeg, plus more for serving

¼ teaspoon ground cinnamon, plus more for serving

⅛ teaspoon ground cloves

Pinch of kosher salt

2 ounces dark rum, plus more as needed

• In a blender, puree the almond milk, avocado, honey, lemon juice, vanilla, nutmeg, cinnamon, cloves, and salt until smooth. Add the rum, and pulse a few more times until combined. Add a bit more rum to taste if desired.

• To serve, split the nog between two glasses and garnish each with a couple of grates of nutmeg or cinnamon.

NOTE: Avocado-Nog is also delicious without the rum, if you are sharing with your younger holiday guests.

AVOCADO BUBBLE TEA

Taiwanese bubble tea, or boba, may be a novelty, but it's a strangely satisfying one. You can make this lightly sweet version without the tapioca pearls, but it won't be nearly as fun. You'll need a wide bubble tea straw to serve.

MAKES TWO 6-OUNCE SERVINGS

¼ cup dried boba tapioca pearls

½ cup brewed black tea, cooled to room temperature

¼ avocado, fresh or frozen and defrosted (see page 13)

½ cup unsweetened almond milk or milk of choice

¼ cup avocado honey or your favorite honey

5 to 6 ice cubes, plus more for serving

• In a medium pot over high heat, bring about 2 cups of water to a boil. Reduce heat to medium high, and cook the tapioca pearls in the boiling water for about 15 minutes, until the pearls soften and are chewy. Drain and rinse the tapioca with cold water.

• While the tapioca is cooling, in a blender, puree the tea, avocado, almond milk, honey, and ice until smooth.

• To serve, split the tapioca between two 10-ounce glasses, add a few ice cubes, and top each glass with the tea mixture.

CADO-RITAS

We make these rocks margaritas by the pitcherful, although the pitcher never stays full for long. Double it and use a punch bowl for a larger group.

MAKES SIX 4-OUNCE SERVINGS

1 cup cold water
¾ cup freshly
   squeezed lime juice
   (from about
   3 large limes)
6 tablespoons sugar
¼ cup diced avocado,
   fresh or frozen and
   defrosted (see
   page 13)
Pinch of kosher salt
1 cup plus 2 table-
   spoons blanco
   tequila

2 ounces orange
   liqueur (like
   Gran Gala)
About ¼ cup Avocado
   Leaf Salt (page 71)
   (optional)
1 or 2 lime wedges,
   for serving
   (optional)
Coarsely broken ice
   cubes, for serving

• In a blender, place the water, lime juice, sugar, avocado, and kosher salt and blend until smooth, and then transfer the liquid to a large pitcher. Cover and refrigerate it for 1 to 10 hours.

• When ready to serve, add the tequila and orange liqueur to the pitcher and stir well to combine.

• To rim your glasses, in a bowl that is a little wider than the 6-ounce rocks glasses you are using, put the avocado leaf salt. Use a lime wedge to wet the edge of each of the six glasses, and dip the top of the glass into the salt. Repeat with the remaining glasses.

• To serve, add ice to the glasses and then split the pitcher between the glasses.

AVOCADO GRASSHOPPER

Jeffrey Morgenthaler, bartender extraordinaire, has revived many classic cocktails, but the grasshopper is my favorite. His version uses ice cream and half-and-half to create a ridiculously delicious shake cocktail. This version skips the dairy entirely, but I don't think you'll miss it, thanks to the thickness of the avocado.

MAKES ONE 6-OUNCE SERVING

1 cup crushed ice
⅓ cup avocado, fresh or frozen and defrosted (see page 13)
⅓ cup unsweetened almond milk or milk of choice
1 ounce vodka
1 ounce crème de menthe
1 ounce crème de cacao
2 teaspoons honey
1 teaspoon Fernet-Branca
Pinch of sea salt
1 sprig fresh mint, for garnish (optional)
1 crushed chocolate wafer cookie, for garnish (optional)

• In a blender on high speed, blend the ice, avocado, almond milk, vodka, crème de menthe, crème de cacao, honey, Fernet, and salt until smooth.

• To serve, pour the cocktail into a tall, frozen glass, and garnish it with the mint and cookie crumbs.

SIPPING CHOCOLATE

This sipping chocolate is about as different from those little packets of cocoa as a macchiato is from a cup of instant coffee. It may be a small serving, but it's full of chocolaty richness, so don't be tempted to fill a typical cocoa mug.

MAKES TWO 6-OUNCE SERVINGS

1 cup unsweetened almond milk or milk of choice, divided

3 tablespoons natural unsweetened cocoa powder

Pinch of ground cinnamon

Pinch of kosher salt

3 tablespoons agave syrup

¼ cup smashed avocado, fresh or frozen and defrosted (see page 13)

NOTE: For an equally delicious but less thick drink, feel free to add more milk.

• In a heavy-bottomed pot over low heat, put about ¼ cup of the almond milk. Whisk in the cocoa powder, cinnamon, and salt until smooth. Add the remaining ¾ cup almond milk and the agave syrup, and stir to combine. Remove the pot from the heat, add the avocado, and then, using an immersion blender, puree the liquid until smooth. Return the pot to the heat and warm the sipping chocolate if needed.

• To serve, divide the sipping chocolate between two small cups.

acknowledgments

A few years ago I was convinced that I'd never write another cookbook. My software start-up was eating up all of my time and energy, and the world of food writing started to revolve more around clickbait than culinary adventuring. As someone who loves the create-and-make part of the job, and loathes anything resembling promoting what I've published, I relegated my blog to the dusty part of the attic that gets looked at with fond memories every now and then, and started saying no to cookbook ideas.

So, for this book, I owe a huge debt of gratitude to my editor Susan Roxborough, who every so often would remind me that writing about food is something I actually love. Every six months or so, I'd get a gentle nudge from her, checking in to see if I had any interest in starting a new book and, in particular, if I had any interest in a book on avocados. For a couple of years, I politely declined, using the (tired old) excuse of I just don't have enough time. Until, finally, she gave me one more little push, and I realized that I was ready. Susan, I'm so glad you stuck with me. After diving deep into avocados during development, I realized how much more I experience and enjoy my food. Every meal becomes a spark of inspiration, and it's a joy. To Susan, and the whole Sasquatch family, thank you so much.

To my recipe checkers, thank you so much for your feedback! A special thanks to Susan Carter for trying out so many recipes!

Thank you to the avocado growers who shared with me such fantastic avocados, especially Michael Fenton from Fenton Family Farm for including such a lovely variety of heirloom avocados and Bailey Brown for the gorgeous sackful of homegrowns.

index

about the author

LARA FERRONI is a tech geek turned food geek who spends her days exploring food and cocktail culture. As a writer and photographer, she can be found learning to make kimchi in the back room of a local church, foraging for wild berries, or snapping away in some of the finest kitchens and bars. She is the author of five cookbooks, including *Doughnuts*, *An Avocado a Day*, *Real Snacks*, and *Put an Egg on It*. You can find more of her tasty photos and recipes on her blog, LaraFerroni.com.

Printed in China
Published by Sasquatch Books
21 20 19 18   9 8 7 6 5 4

Editor: Susan Roxborough | Production editor: Emma Reh | Photographs: Lara Ferroni
Design: Anna Goldstein | Copyeditor: Michelle Hope Anderson

Library of Congress Cataloging-in-Publication Data
Names: Ferroni, Lara, author.
Title: An avocado a day : more than 70 recipes for enjoying nature's most
   delicious superfood / Lara Ferroni.
Description: Seattle, WA : Sasquatch Books, [2016] | Includes bibliographical
   references and index.
Identifiers: LCCN 2016025792 | ISBN 9781632170811 (alk. paper)
Subjects: LCSH: Cooking (Avocado) | LCGFT: Cookbooks.
Classification: LCC TX813.A9 F47 2016 | DDC 641.6/4653--dc23
LC record available at https://lccn.loc.gov/2016025792

ISBN: 978-1-63217-081-1

Sasquatch Books | 1904 Third Avenue, Suite 710 | Seattle, WA 98101
(206) 467-4300 | www.sasquatchbooks.com

conversions

VOLUME

UNITED STATES	METRIC	IMPERIAL
¼ tsp.	1.25 ml	
½ tsp.	2.5 ml	
1 tsp.	5 ml	
½ Tbsp.	7.5 ml	
1 Tbsp.	15 ml	
⅛ c.	30 ml	1 fl. oz.
¼ c.	60 ml	2 fl. oz.
⅓ c.	80 ml	2.5 fl. oz.
½ c.	125 ml	4 fl. oz.
1 c.	250 ml	8 fl. oz.
2 c. (1 pt.)	500 ml	16 fl. oz.
1 qt.	1 l	32 fl. oz.

LENGTH

UNITED STATES	METRIC
⅛ in.	3 mm
¼ in.	6 mm
½ in.	1.25 cm
1 in.	2.5 cm
1 ft.	30 cm

WEIGHT

AVOIRDUPOIS	METRIC
¼ oz.	7 g
½ oz.	15 g
1 oz.	30 g
2 oz.	60 g
3 oz.	90 g
4 oz.	115 g
5 oz.	150 g
6 oz.	175 g
7 oz.	200 g
8 oz. (½ lb.)	225 g
9 oz.	250 g
10 oz.	300 g
11 oz.	325 g
12 oz.	350 g
13 oz.	375 g
14 oz.	400 g
15 oz.	425 g
16 oz. (1 lb.)	450 g
1½ lb.	750 g
2 lb.	900 g
2¼ lb.	1 kg
3 lb.	1.4 kg
4 lb.	1.8 kg

TEMPERATURE

OVEN MARK	FAHRENHEIT	CELSIUS	GAS
Very cool	250–275	130–140	½–1
Cool	300	150	2
Warm	325	165	3
Moderate	350	175	4
Moderately hot	375	190	5
	400	200	6
Hot	425	220	7
	450	230	8
Very Hot	475	245	9